Advance Praise for
THE WORDS WE CHOOSE

"I have spent much of my professional life refining communications in healthcare to advance safety, connection, collaboration, gratitude and valuing those we care for and work with. Terre's work in *The Words We Choose* took me to a totally new level! It is an immensely practical guide for the day-to-day conversations that allow relationships to blossom, connections to deepen, and cultures to mature. Whether you are a clinician with a patient, a leader to a team, a parent to a child or communicating with a stranger, the words we choose can change everything in these moments. I am better for reading Terre's work, and challenged with all of the blind spots she helped me see. As a constant student of communication, I am immensely grateful to have a whole new toolkit in *The Words We Choose*." —**STEPHEN BEESON, M.D.** - Founder of the Clinician Experience Project, Author of *Practicing Excellence, A Physician Manual to Exceptional Healthcare* and *Engaging Physician, A Manual to Physician Partnership*

"This is an important book in our evolution to a more heart-centered world. Terre eloquently brings to life how words can cage us in or set us free. This book does a beautiful job of unlocking the reality we create through the power of our words - step by step. I love the simplicity - and importance - of the message she shares. Terre slows down our thinking so we can 'hear' the deeper meaning behind what we say. Truly profound - what a gift to the world! I cannot wait to recommend the book to clients across the globe." —**KIMBERLY FAITH** - Award-Winning Author, Futurist, & Systems Thinking Expert

"*The Words We Choose* is a timely examination of how words mold our emotions and shape our relationships with the world." —**KARL VANDEVENDER, M.D.**, Chief Physician, HCA Leadership Institute

"I learned by reading *The Words We Choose* that we typically speak 16,000 words a day, aside from what we type into emails and texts. That presents a lot of opportunities for our words to be disconnected from our values and intentions. This book explores how to ensure we choose our words wisely in a myriad of situations and in a way that benefits all. I found the chapter on words at work particularly valuable because it provided great insight and pragmatic advice on how to use words to unite ourselves and our teams together in our common purpose. It is filled with practical applications, reflections and stories that reinforce the concepts." —**CHARLENE LI** - Author of 6 books, including recent bestseller, *The Disruption Mindset*, Senior Fellow at Altimeter, a Prophet Company

THE WORDS WE CHOOSE

Your Guide to How and Why Words Matter

TERRE SHORT

Epigraph Books
Rhinebeck, New York

Paperback ISBN 978-1-951937-52-2
eBook ISBN 978-1-951937-53-9

Library of Congress Control Number 2020913488

Book registration number TXu002186929

Excerpts and modified excerpts from *Spiritual Rebel* by Sarah Bowen (2019), published by Monkfish Book Publishing Company, Rhinebeck New York are used here by kind permission.

Book design by Colin Rolfe

Epigraph Books
22 East Market Street, Suite 304
Rhinebeck, NY 12572
(845) 876-4861
epigraphps.com

To all those I have learned from, and will learn from,
along my evolutionary path.

Contents

Prologue

As I put the finishing touches on this book, I am learning how a global pandemic (COVID-19) affects communication while paying close attention to the word choices of world leaders and how these choices define them. I am witnessing global connections that fill my heart with hope alongside images so grim that words will never be able to fully capture the heartache. "At a loss for words" is an understatement that gives way to a silence that can become deafening. As communities embrace "lockdowns" and "physical distancing," I believe we are learning just how much we rely on words to shape our world and feed our souls.

While navigating a global pandemic, America is at the same time confronting a much older and perhaps more dangerous affliction: Systemic racism. Ahmaud Arbery, Breonna Taylor, and George Floyd have become household names. The power of words is especially poignant, and painful, as the Black community implores Americans to recognize the deaths of these individuals, and so many more, as murders inextricably connected to the country's long history of racism. George Floyd's death at the hands of a policeman has inspired national civil rights protests and suddenly the voices of all races, ethnicities and ages are collectively calling for abolishing systemic racism in all its forms and at all levels.

Resources abound for educating individuals on our role in bridging the gaps between individual realities, social justice and true equality for all. Some of the people I reference in the racism section in Chapter Three have been at the forefront of this critical conversation. Sustained and meaningful change hinges on our ability to reach beyond the words we choose into actions that serve the greater good of all. For those with inherent privilege due to race or identity in a majority group, this will require a deeper and perhaps different understanding of the history that brought a country like America to a place of inequality, and the related individual and collective reckoning being asked of us. My deep hope is that Mr. Floyd's final words, "I can't breathe!" have propelled the energy and commitment needed for the required paradigm shift.

"We're creating the world by how we speak to each other."
TOM KENYON

Introduction

The very first friend to read a chapter of this book returned the marked-up pages with a note that made me cry. She told me a story of how she had interacted with a stranger online and how she had paused long enough to consider her word choices. In the moment, she recalled what she had read about connecting words to values. She examined her intent as well as the impact to the recipient. It ends up this was a great move, as she then learned this person lives and works in her same small town. She was planning to meet her in person and engage in a heart-to-heart conversation.

Every time we express ourselves through words, we have an opportunity to connect our thoughts with what we feel in our hearts. Our words matter. As we see from the above anecdote from my friend, by pausing to consider her words, she was able to make a connection that now extends beyond that initial meeting. If I consider my emotional state first, I can contemplate how this thought feels and if it aligns with my values and my intention. Once aligned, my words will come from my heart with the intention of connecting with emotional sincerity to the other person. I do not suggest this in a "woo-woo" way. I suggest this as the only way — in business, with your family, online, with your neighbor, and when you connect to a higher power.

Have you ever felt misunderstood? Does saying the wrong thing frustrate you? Whether it is knowing what to say to someone who is grieving, someone from another culture, to a non-binary individual, or responding in difficult work or family situations, you can speak in a way that truly represents you and impacts the other person as you intend.

Lifelong learners, life explorers, parents, tenured and developing leaders will all benefit from the suggestions, stories, activities and reflections in this book. You can transform your communication through the power of your words.

In these pages, I will explore how our most important word choices are those we tell ourselves. I dig into how to choose words wisely with loved ones, as some of these word choices may influence a lifetime. I examine how we communicate in the world at large, including having the last word, habitual words, words that represent belief-limiting isms (racism, sexism, ageism), identity-specific suggestions, slang, loss and grief, and with those struggling with alcoholism or substance abuse. The chapter on words we use at work spans effective recognition, being of service, communicating as a leader, clinical settings, and difficult conversations. I explore word use beyond speaking, such as text messages, emails, written notes, and when we engage in social media. The final chapter invites you to consider how you use words to connect to the universe. This could be through prayer, meditation, a spiritual practice, or religious tradition.

You will improve your self-awareness and build upon your emotional intelligence. Along the way, you will learn to fully contemplate your intention in each situation. You will develop keywords that align with your values and keep you connected to them. You will become an expert at owning the words you choose and routinely choosing them wisely.

I will not cover word use from a grammatical standpoint. There will be no admonishment for when you use "I" or "me" and whether you end a sentence with a preposition. If I offer words that are currently not in your vocabulary, I encourage you to consider if they benefit you. I have challenged myself to appeal to all generations and trust you to relate in a manner that works best for you. I also intend for the content to apply to all people regardless of their gender. When I speak about individuals, I alternate between "him" and "her."

I have coached communication for decades. Although my master's degree is in business administration, not linguistics, I am a life-long learner who devours material on personal growth. I have always been in the people business and therefore compelled to learn how to communicate effectively. This serves my coaching/consulting/speaking business where I specialize in leadership development. I learn from my leadership experience, as well as from my clients whose businesses vary greatly. I have been a leader in hospitality and health-care. I have owned and overseen a wide range of start-ups including fitness, baby boomer marketing, fiber arts, internet marketing, luxury resort operations, and medical staffing.

I draw on world travels and have resided in six states and two countries, outside the United States. I have traveled to all fifty states and enjoy exploring cultural differences. Differences in values and beliefs drive variations on word choices. I have coached and consulted throughout the United States, as well as several foreign countries. As importantly, I am the mother of "twenty-somethings," a son and a daughter, who teach me daily. My husband is a very enlightened man who happily explores the impact of word choices within family dynamics.

While this book is not a substitute for effective one-on-one coaching, it is filled with examples, exercises, and reflections that will grow your communication skills. Packed with research, this book endeavors to cover most common communication opportunities. However, some of the sections could be, and should be, standalone books. I note resources to serve your deeper exploration.

An individual speaks an average of 16,000 words each day (Mehl, 2007). This represents a lot of daily word choices. This does not include words typed into an email, text, or otherwise written. Our daily experiences are shaped by words spoken to and by us. What impact did your words have today? Did they serve you well? Did they serve another? Yours is the voice of humankind. I hope my work will support you using your words for the good of all.

I invite you to continue reading to enhance your ability to consistently communicate intentionally. I hope you will engage in the reflections and activities that amplify the concepts. I challenge you to choose your words from your heart in order to connect to the heart of another in all situations.

Tips for navigating this book:

This icon indicates when to pause and engage your heart in a reflection.

This icon prompts you to dive into an activity to work through your own examples.

This icon signals a story to reinforce how words matter.

"It does indeed matter what we do, say, and even think.
Everything counts, everything leaves an imprint in our minds."
PEMA CHODRON

Chapter ONE

WORDS THAT CONNECT US TO OURSELVES

Lead with Values — Your WHY

"What do you know about writing a book? What will you write about?" my mother asks. Hmmm, does she have a point? My first thought is how others in my professional life describe me as a good communicator, extremely organized and efficient, and noticeably confident. I value these characteristics. I wonder why these traits have abandoned me when the voice in my head sends doubtful messages at various times of the day and night about my ability to write a book. Where have my words of confidence gone?

The words I choose for myself lay the foundation for my communication with others. They also guide what I do daily, what is important to me, and how I contribute to the world. If I choose words of doubt and sabotage, I may not be able to get out of bed in the morning. If I surround myself with others who choose a negative perspective, this will challenge my daily activity as well. My internal heart-to-heart conversations must always revolve around my values in order to truly represent me.

Everything you do and say represents your values, what you believe in, and who you are. We become uncentered, or off-kilter, when our words do not align with our values. When this happens, we find ourselves feeling misunderstood or unable to connect with others as intended. The words we choose reflect our values and intent. How often do we reflect on the impact our words have on others? How do we reconcile the impact of our words and our intent, and confirm that they align with our values? All of this typically occurs in the nano-second between a thought and the expression of that thought – verbally, texted, or written.

As mentioned in the introduction, the world would be a better place if all conversations were framed as heart to heart. When you do this, you align with your values – that which is in your heart. You will also be honoring the impact you have on the recipient of your words. Even what I refer to as "alleged difficult conversations" will be easier for you and well received by others. (See Chapter Four.)

To assess how well words align with values, values need to be named and tested for relevance. In her book, *Dare to Lead*, Brené Brown provides a chapter on how to clarify and name your values. She offers this definition, "A value is a way of being or believing that we hold most important." (Brown, 2018). *Psychology Today* offers a six-step process online for determining your personal core values. The article provides prompts and reflection exercises to ensure the reader does not simply choose from an existing list (Selig, 2018). If you have not recently assessed your personal values, doing so will set you up for choosing words that will represent your values.

Most people have very vague senses of their personal values. There might be values they feel they *should* have, ones influenced by society and culture. A true discovery of personal values can be guided by a professional coach and includes honest reflection. The process includes reflection on experiences and beliefs, and an exploration of your basic needs and sense of fulfillment. Without clarity of your core values, it will be difficult to communicate in a way that represents who you are.

VALUES EXERCISE:

Steps	Example	Your Answers
1. Read your last two texts, your last two emails, and review your last two conversations (not just what you said, but the words you chose to say).	*Conversation reflection: I thanked my husband for making me lunch, or I said, "Thanks for lunch, honey."*	
2. Note all words that may reflect a value.	*Thanks, honey*	
3. Identify the value(s) you were communicating.	*Gratitude, family*	
4. Choose better words – ones that align perfectly with your values. Contemplate the impact of the change.	*"Thanks for lunch, I appreciate you." This equates to a stronger emphasis on my value of gratitude*	
5. Weave these words into your day and practice!		

REFLECTION

Three of my values are honesty, clarity and efficiency. Occasionally, to be efficient, my communication lacks clarity. In my brevity, it is possible I omit something that keeps me from presenting an idea or thought honestly. **Has this happened to you? Which of your values typically takes precedence?**

"Have to" or "Get to"

A dad picks up one child from school and ends up late for the game of another child. He is likely to say to the second child (Sam), "I'm sorry Sam, I had to pick up Sally." Who does this lay the blame on? How might this make Sally and Sam feel? What the dad believes he values is being there for his kids. What he is messaging is that it is hard to juggle their schedules and that doing something for one causes him to slight the other. It is unlikely this is his intent. If he wants to lead with his value of being there for his kids he might say, "Sam, I got to pick up Sally today and I am sorry that my timing was such that we are a bit late for your game. I love your games and watching you play."

Commonly, we speak in terms of what we "have" to do instead of what we "get" to do. "Having" to do something implies a burden or obligation. So often what we are referring to "having" to do is quite far from a burden. Additionally, this impacts those we converse with, especially if they feel a part of the perceived burden of what you "have" to do.

REFLECTION

Nurse says to a colleague, "I have to care for Mrs. Klein today."

Reflections for you:

- When Mrs. Klein overhears this, how does she feel?
- What value does this represent on behalf of the nurse?
- What value do you think really represents the nurse?
- How would saying, "I get to care for Mrs. Klein today" change things? For Mrs. Klein and for the RN?
- How do facial expressions and body language influence the impact of the words?

I had the privilege of coaching Mike Baxter and his healthcare leaders. At the time, Mike was the CEO of Parkview Health Systems. One of Mike's values was being of service and he exemplified this in his leadership style. Most notably, he comfortably spoke in terms of what he and his team "got" to do on a daily basis, as opposed to what they "had" to do. I heard him many times, in addressing both leaders and staff, frame his message around what he and his leaders had the privilege to share. For example, he might say, "We get to review our discharge process in order to ensure it is beneficial to our patients and clinicians." He lived his values as CEO in how he expressed himself and always led with how he and his team got to be of service to others – patients, staff, clinicians, and the community. Mike took great care to set the context for his communication. He knew that feeling his audience was as important as how he made them feel with the words he chose.

When staff and leaders constantly hear what they "have" to do they are less likely to feel ownership in a process or plan. Speaking in these terms is directive and oftentimes does not include *why* you requested an action. It can also lead to a victim mentality, as one feels like the passive recipient of orders. It is counterintuitive to feel that having to do something aligns with one's values. "Getting" to do something because it aligns with values and typically comes with an explanation of *why*, however, is relatable. It is amazing how this simple change in words creates space for more positivity and commitment. Let us explore some examples.

ACTIVITY

How do you feel when you hear the following statements? Here are some choices: Empowered/disempowered, positive/negative, inspired/unmotivated, included/excluded, excited/indifferent.

Value	Have to Statement	Feeling	Get to Statement	Feeling
Teamwork	You have to clock in no more than 10 minutes early.		You get to clock in up to 10 minutes early.	
Communication	You have to tell your team about the new dining hours.		You get to tell your team about the new dining hours.	
Service	We have to serve 10 customers an hour in order to meet our service goals.		We get to serve 10 customers an hour in order to meet our service goals.	
Honesty	We have to tell the parents why we are changing this policy.		We get to tell the parents why we are changing this policy and how it will impact them.	

Sometimes words do not align with one's values. Occasionally, saying anything at all is unnecessary. It is helpful to ask, *what purpose does this serve?* If the conversation you wish to have serves your purpose and values, then that is a great start. If it serves only you, a next step would be to consider the impact to the others. If it serves no purpose to share a comment, it is better left unsaid. For example: When our elders are forgetful and we tell them something for a fourth time, we may be inclined to add, "This is the fourth time I told you this." It may support my value of being efficient (and only doing things once) and my purpose of letting them know we have discussed this. However, chances are good there will be a fifth time; mentioning this being the fourth may serve to make them feel inadequate, troublesome, a burden, angry with themselves, or "D" – all of the above. It is unlikely this was your intent or that this outcome serves your values.

Let us consider when intent conflicts with values. Have you ever intended to hurt someone? Your immediate response is likely "no." I assure you most of us occasionally choose words that intend to hurt or to make someone feel bad. This could be due to them hurting you, you wanting to make a point, or you feeling overwhelmed by a certain issue and are therefore lashing out – wanting the other to know what it feels like. There are a myriad of reasons why we choose words that hurt. Oftentimes, we only need to pause to reflect on values and intent and to check in on our heart's message. Consider *why* this conversation is important. Contemplation can take a nano-second if you are aware of your values.

Emotional Intelligence and Self-Esteem

Volumes exist on Emotional Intelligence (EI). The literature supports the correlation between high Emotional Intelligence and effective leadership. Emotional Intelligence also informs parenting styles and relationship patterns. There is no doubt that Emotional Intelligence affects the words chosen in various conversations. The five components of Emotional Intelligence are self-awareness, self-regulation, motivation, empathy, and social skills.

Here are the key definitions of Emotional Intelligence (Harvard Business Review, 2015):
- Self-awareness: The ability to recognize and understand your moods, emotions, and drives, as well as their effect on others.
- Self-regulation: The ability to control or redirect disruptive impulses and moods. The propensity to suspend judgment – to think before acting.

- Motivation: A passion to work for reasons that go beyond money or status. Propensity to pursue goals with energy and persistence.
- Empathy: The ability to understand the emotional make-up of other people. Skill in treating people according to their emotional reactions.
- Social skill: Proficiency in managing relationships and building networks. And ability to find common ground and build rapport.

One critical component here is the understanding and control of emotion. How well you manage your own emotions and energy and how well you read the emotions and energy of others will have an impact on the words you choose. It is best to check in on emotional triggers and get your energy around a sensitive issue in check before choosing *any* words. Your next step would be a quick assessment of the person you are conversing with. You have probably heard the phrase "treat with kid gloves," which means tread carefully in a conversation. This reflects a sense that the other person has some emotion or elevated energy around a topic or in general. This consideration (of treating with kid gloves) is Emotional Intelligence in action. The tricky part is when doing so compromises your values and therefore your sense of self. This directs us back to the self-awareness component of Emotional Intelligence.

Multiple studies in the last 20 years explore the relationship between Emotional Intelligence and self-esteem. Schutte et al's work in "cognition and emotion" found that higher Emotional Intelligence is associated with higher self-esteem. Mixed models of Emotional Intelligence have emerged in addition to those outlined above. The following competencies may also factor into Emotional Intelligence: Emotional literacy, self-regard, self-management, self-motivation, change resilience, interpersonal relations, and the integration of head and heart (Schutte, 2002) (Coetzee, 2006).

The literature supports that Emotional Intelligence develops over the course of one's life. The following books offer guidance on how to improve one's Emotional Intelligence (Harvard Business Review, 2018) (Greaves, 2009):

- Everyday Emotional Intelligence – Harvard Business Review
- Emotional Intelligence 2.0 – Travis Bradberry and Jean Greaves

Many of the strategies outlined in these books boil down to either how you communicate with others or how you manage your internal communication. This all gets back to the words we choose. The good news is that Emotional Intelligence can improve at any age. All you need is the desire to take a closer look at yourself. After considerable research, I offer the following key strategies and illustrate how they relate to the words you choose.

Self-Awareness: The best way to reconcile how you *believe* people perceive you with how you are truly perceived is to ask. This includes asking others as well as yourself some important questions. Here are some sample questions:

Self:
- Why did I just do or say that?
- Have I had this reaction in the past? If so, how is it different this time?
- Why is that important to me?
- How do those words or actions relate to my values?
- Were are my actions or words respectful?
- What would I call that emotion?
- What am I feeling right now?
- Why am I feeling this way?
- What might I have done differently or better?
- Would I use different words in a future similar situation? What would they be?
- Who can provide me with candid feedback?

Others:
- Did you perceive any emotion when I was speaking?
- What type of emotion did I exhibit?
- How did the words I used impact you?
- Did you perceive that my words aligned with my values?
- When I communicate, is it clear what my values are?
- Can you give me a specific example of how I act when I am sad? Happy? Frustrated? Excited?

Self-regulation or self-management: The key here is having control of your self-talk. There are many other important strategies such as getting plenty of rest, surrounding yourself with supportive people, continually appreciating lessons learned and a positive, confident perspective. Although there is an entire section in this book dedicated to the voice in your head, here are a few key words and phrases that relate to improving self-regulation.
- What sort of pause would serve me now? Count to 10, take a walk, return tomorrow?
- Check in with your internal voice and try these prompts: My emotional wellbeing is important. I value being in control of my emotions. Overreacting serves no purpose. I am enough, more than enough, smart enough, strong enough, capable of managing my emotions.
- Identify the difference between an emotional and a rational reaction and outline the value in each.

Social skills and relationship management: If this does not come easily for you, don't worry; there is much to read on this topic. The basis of this skill lies in the power of observation. Having great radar is key. Every day presents the opportunity to observe others. You can observe them in your work environment, at the movies, and in your home. As you observe, you can contemplate the following:

- What is body language telling me?
- What do I read in facial expressions and eye contact?
- What powerful words are used? What impact do these words have?
- What questions do I have prepared to share in a social setting? Here are a few examples:
  - What are you currently working on? What was the best part of this week for you?
  - What is your favorite outdoor activity?
  - What is the best book you have read this past year?
- Tap into your sympathy which is quite different from empathy. Sympathy is how you feel as a reflection of what another has shared with you. It is about you but may be helpful to the other. Tapping into your empathy is even better – see below.
- TLTTHITN = The Last Thing They Hear is Their Name. I learned this from Stan Bromley, one of Four Season Hotel's greatest hoteliers. I used to coach this in hospitality, though it is relevant for most businesses and certainly in clinical settings. Using the name of the person you are speaking with is a simple effort and goes a long way in building and managing a relationship – even a brief one. Consider what not retaining a name you learned moments earlier says about your emotional investment in the conversation. If you know this is a personal challenge, you might consider reviewing some of the tips in *The Memory Book* by Harry Lorayne & Jerry Lucas (Lucas, 1975). This resource is a gem. Although published in 1975, I have used the tips for recalling names in my coaching for decades.

Motivation: In the context of Emotional Intelligence, this refers to your general motivation as an individual. Here are a few suggestions for keeping your level of motivation healthy.

- Make your goals public – use extremely specific words of commitment.
- Assess your challenges regularly – are there enough of them, too many?
- Consider your response to challenges – do you remain optimistic? Can you see the silver lining in adversity?
- Consider all change to be a form of continuous improvement – such as the work you do personally to improve a component of your Emotional Intelligence.

Empathy: Daniel Goleman offers three distinct kinds of empathy. Each of these will have an impact on the words you choose. Your level of empathy is circumstantial and is something to continually assess (Harvard Business Review, 2015).

- Cognitive empathy: The ability to understand another person's perspective.
- Emotional empathy: The ability to feel what someone else feels.
- Empathetic concern: Ability to sense what another person needs from you.

To gauge and strengthen your level of empathy, consider the following reflections:

- Having good self-awareness and social awareness to begin with helps further develop empathy. This includes the ability to place yourself firmly in the shoes of another and to use your powers of observation to take in the whole picture, including the emotions of others.
- Assess your listening skills. Are you hearing more than what is spoken? Do you hear a feeling?
- Speak in terms of what you hear, indicating that you understand what the person is going through.
- Show concern in practical ways by asking, "Have you thought

about how you could...?" or "What would be most helpful now?"

- Pause and determine if you truly feel the impact of being in the other person's shoes. Can you relate? If not, how can you support him? Be authentic about your willingness and desire to fully understand and be supportive.

Why does this self-reflection matter? Let us take a deeper look. Marshall Rosenberg, a prominent psychologist who spoke and wrote on nonviolent communication, explains that there are basically two things that bring people joy. The first is to gain joy from the suffering of others, which leads to violent communication or simply violence. The second way an individual gains joy is by improving the wellbeing of others, which leads to compassionate communication. He traced this back 8,000 years to when a domination society began. When there are levels of perceived superiority, a language of judgment and classification evolves. This language of domination serves to dehumanize others. Luckily, Rosenberg and some well-known paleontologists believe that this has been an evolutionary snap that we find ourselves stuck in. They also believe that we are moving towards a needs-based and therefore, more compassionate society. Rosenberg contends that communication is born out of needs. In the domination framework, communication focuses on justifying one's position, and this is really an expression of unmet needs (Rosenberg, 2003).

In his work to bridge communication gaps, Rosenberg often asked the following questions: How did you enrich another person today? What needs were met? How did this make you feel? Do you know of anything more fulfilling?

It seems the tie to superiority is as ingrained as our fight or flight response. Fortunately, as homo sapiens, we can contemplate and adjust our perceptions. This is the first step in recognizing bias and underlying beliefs that may influence the words we choose.

This also brings us to a deeper look at Emotional Intelligence. Many people feel that self-awareness, the ability to understand one's emotions, is the most important component of Emotional Intelligence. People with this strength continually assess their strengths and weaknesses and work on any areas in need of improvement. Self-awareness is the key to changing your story and therefore the voice in your head. Once you are aware of your strengths, it is much easier to lean on them when negativity presents.

Self-regulation, the ability to control emotions and impulses, is the next step. With self-regulation, feelings such as anger, jealousy, impulsiveness, and thoughtfulness are managed. The third component is motivation, which people with a high degree of Emotional Intelligence naturally exhibit. They are very productive, appreciate a good challenge, and are effective in their endeavors. Empathy is the fourth component and typically thought of as the second most important one. This strength leads to the ability to understand the viewpoints of others as well as their needs and wants. Empaths are not quick to judge and they communicate openly and honestly. Listening well is a part of being empathetic. Lastly, someone with high Emotional Intelligence has superior social skills. This enables her to build and maintain relationships by leveraging her excellent communication skills.

Understanding your level of Emotional Intelligence is as foundational as understanding your core values if you desire to communicate well. There are simple and quick online tests that provide reliable results. You can search online for "Emotional Intelligence tests." Once you know your score in the five areas, you can determine your strengths and weaknesses and therefore your areas of opportunity. As mentioned above, a good starting point would be self-awareness. Reading this book is a solid step in the direction of improving one's self-awareness. Next, you can build a plan to improve on one or two areas over a few months, using some of the suggestions above. Most importantly, determine from your score where you are at risk of choosing words unwisely. This could be in social settings, or at work due to low motivation scores. One option is to engage a coach who can help you on your journey to improve your Emotional Intelligence over time. Doing so will impact both your internal and external voice and benefit you greatly.

In Christopher Mruk's second edition of *Self Esteem*, he outlines the construct of self-esteem as it relates to worthiness and competence. He refers to the development of self-esteem before ages four to five as pre-esteem and he refers to middle childhood as, "an unforgiving place by comparison. The child's sense of worthiness, growing confidence, and developing a sense of individuality all play important roles in shaping his or her perception and experience. Consequently, past experiences with being valued or competent (or, conversely, being rejected or incompetent) influence how the child perceives risk, evaluates chances, determines his or her level of motivation, and so on." (Mruk, 1999).

Additionally, all of John Gottman's work promotes a feedback ratio of 5:1, positive to negative. Gottman has been at this for decades and in 2002, he decoded key communication factors that lead to divorce in his study with Robert Levinson. They found the main factor to successful relationships to be a consistent use of positive over negative reinforcement, by a factor of five. (Gottman, 2002). This confirms the need to choose words wisely and with good intentions, as well as the frequency needed to truly provide positive reinforcement.

These important studies beg consideration of nature versus nurture, as well as who is involved in the nurture part. Most adults I know have childhood stories they believe have shaped them. Some of these stories take place in their families and some at school with friends. Some are positive and some are negative and have had a related impact to the person's psyche. Some people choose to hold onto stories that negatively impact their self-esteem. Others change their narratives altogether and excel beyond expectations. The narratives show up as the voice in his or her head. And the voice is a choice.

The Voice is a Choice

I would like to propose that collectively we start to replace judgment with witness. It is much more productive for each of us to show up fully present and ready to witness, as opposed to judge. This includes how we witness our own actions and reactions. If we are present as witnesses, how does that inform the narrative? I own the narrative playing in my head. I own the words that represent me inside and outside my head. It serves my values and intent better to continually bear witness to them, as opposed to judging them, which can create a vicious cycle of negativity. The same holds true for any judgment from others. This makes me think of one of my favorite Eleanor Roosevelt quotes, "What other people think of me is none of my business."

Michael Singer does a fantastic job in *The Untethered Soul* of exploring the voice inside your head. He poses powerful questions to help you reduce the voice that proposes negativity and holds you back. His simple approach confirms the reality that we are each in control of the voices in our heads and supports how to equip the voices with what we need to hear. When "the voice" undermines our goals, does not support our dreams, or holds us back in any way, we need to challenge why this is the case. We must contemplate why we allow beliefs to form words that we hear over and over in our heads that do not align with our values (Singer, 2007).

Let us first explore the difference between values and beliefs. Beliefs influence values and values influence behaviors. Values guide day-to-day choices and support a sense of right versus wrong. Values can vary greatly from person to person and change for individuals over time. They are abstract guiding principles that shape how we experience the world. Beliefs are assumptions, not based on fact, but oftentimes founded in past experiences. In psychology, beliefs are the foundation of our conscience. Very powerful beliefs exist in religion that have a direct impact on individual values. Beliefs may cause biases and at times beliefs or values may be in conflict. All of this affects the voice in your head and the words that voice chooses.

Let us pull this all together in an example. I have created a story based on some assumptions. This is not my story and it does not necessarily represent my values and beliefs.

ASSUMPTIONS

My religion professes that a lesbian relationship is wrong and I believe in my religion and all of its teachings.

1. I have two teenagers and I teach them about inclusivity and loving others. We speak often about our value of kindness and how this can combat bullying.
2. I pray daily to be strong in my values of authenticity, kindness, generosity, honesty, and family.
3. My friend tells me that the new Physical Education teacher is a lesbian.

The voice in my head goes crazy. I hear it say things like:

- *How could the school have allowed this?*
- *What if the children find out? What if they already know? How will this affect them?*
- *This is a Christian school!*
- *If we must have a lesbian teacher, wouldn't English be better, not a class where they are changing clothes?*
- *What will the church say about this?*

All along, the voice is coming from my **beliefs**; it has yet to tap in to my values. When, or if, it does, I hear things like:

- *I am still going to be kind to this person.*
- *I am going to be honest with the children about this; they need to know.*
- *I must protect the children; we will discuss this as a family.*
- *I will pray about this and know what to do next.*

- *I am just going to be myself and treat her like anyone else. I can do this.*
- *God is testing me.*

In this example, my beliefs and my values are in conflict. There are words the voice in my head has chosen that have an impact on how I am interpreting this conflict. Here is an **interpretation** of the impact some of the words may have:

- *How could the **school** have **allowed** this?* I am not responsible; I am blaming others.
- *What if the children **find out**? What if they already know? How will this **affect them**?* I am not owning my value of honesty and authenticity or I would not have such worries.
- *This is a Christian school!* I expect others to support my values and my beliefs.
- *If we **must have** a lesbian teacher, wouldn't English be better, not a class where they are changing clothes?* I have moved into assumptions supported by my beliefs and somehow think the new teacher will influence my children differently than other teachers based solely on their sexual orientation.
- *What will **the church** say about this?* This situation is beyond me and therefore I only have so much ownership in this conflict.
- *I am **still** going to be kind to this person.* This is the first step in establishing my bias – my kindness will require an effort, beyond what other individuals require of me.
- *I am going to be **honest** with the children about this; they need to know.* My honesty will be measured and not offered to the full depth of what my children deserve.
- *I must **protect** the children; we will discuss this as a family.* My value of family supports this discussion, but my beliefs may guide the conversation and enhance my bias.
- *I am just going to be myself and **treat her like anyone else**. I can do this.* Another step in establishing my bias – I will need to

make a conscious attempt to live by my value of kindness with this individual.

- *God is testing me.* Again, I only have partial ownership in this – it is beyond my capabilities.

How could my words serve me better in this scenario? I need to own the voice in my head and guide the voice with my values, and potentially reassess my beliefs. It all may sound like this (most impactful words highlighted) when I change my words TO:

- *How could the **school** have **allowed** this?* TO: **I am responsible** for **how I respond** to this information and to this new person.
- *What if the children **find out**? What if they already know? How will this **affect them**?* TO: I **own my value** of honesty and authenticity and I will help the kids understand this **from a place of kindness**. This will be a **valuable conversation for all of us**.
- *This is a Christian school!* TO: I **support and will live my values** and may need to assess my beliefs.
- *If we **must have** a lesbian teacher, wouldn't English be better, not a class where they are changing clothes?* TO: **I trust** that my children are not treated any differently based on the new teacher's sexual orientation, nor would we ever treat this teacher any differently than any others.
- *What will **the church** say about this?* TO: My values may conflict with the beliefs of the church and that is okay, I will find strength in prayer and **continue to connect with my values**.
- *I am **still** going to be kind to this person.* TO: I am unsure what difference this news makes and why it even matters. My **kindness extends to all** regardless if their beliefs or sexual orientation is different than mine.
- *I am going to be **honest** with the children about this; they need to know.* TO: I am looking forward to the opportunity to **discuss this openly and honestly** with the children.
- *I must **protect** the children; we will discuss this as a family.* TO:

My family **value is strong** and has served me well; we will **all benefit** from this discussion.

- *I am just going to be myself and **treat her like anyone else**. I can do this.* TO: Living my value of kindness means I treat everyone with **equal kindness**; this would never require any different energy or effort.

- *God is testing me.* TO: **My values and beliefs** are frequently tested, which is why I have them – to **guide me**, even in conflict.

I encourage you to consider how your past might influence your perspective. People do not like to think that they are biased or that underlying beliefs control their subconscious. However, this is very difficult to dispute. I am a white woman of privilege and until the last few years, I did not fully understand how this might influence my subconscious. This affects the story that I tell myself — the voice in my head, as well as how I relate to others. I have recognized that my words and actions sometimes serve to overcompensate for my position of privilege. This includes how I relate to indigenous people, as well as people of color. If I listen closely, I can hear myself trying to make up for the wrongs of my ancestors. I believe this influences the words I choose, just as I believe it influences the words of those born into different circumstances.

The voice in your head has incredible power. We must continually be a witness to that power and consciously choose to change the narrative when appropriate. This following story has been shared by a dear friend, who was initially shaken by the narrative she witnessed her son believing.

STORY: A CONCERNED MOM

Doubt. Overlooked. Unappreciated. Defeated. Conformed. Sad. Lonely.

My mind grew numb as I heard these words from my sweet son after his spring semester of his freshman year at college. As his mother, I was shocked. Shocked that someone so incredible could actually think this about himself. Shocked that the picture shown to everyone on the outside obviously was something very different than what was actually believed on the inside. Shocked and sad that I had, as his mother, missed it.

But the change we witnessed over the next months was even more amazing and miraculous. Yes, his dad and I were right there with him each step of the way, but we could not solve this for him. He had to do this one himself.

It has been said, *"When writing the story of your life, don't let anyone else hold the pen."*

And this is what he did. He recognized his weakness, asked for help, realized the narrative in his head was not true, grabbed the pen, and started writing his own story. He changed by changing the narrative that was continually playing over and over in his head.

The weeks that followed were not easy, but the steps were intentional. Instead of hiding, he was renewing and making new positive relationships. Instead of being a victim, he started to serve others less fortunate here in the States and abroad. He renewed his faith and belief in God and his purpose for Him. He changed his location and goals. He started writing and journaling positive experiences and thoughts.

And guess what happened? The words started to change in his head. As the words changed, so did his story. People started to notice the difference.

Just recently, he came home on break with a group of college friends. As we sat around the family dinner table, I sat back and listened as he and his friends laughed hysterically, told stories about each other and just enjoyed life together. As we were cleaning up the dishes, I said to him, "You really seem happy." He looked at me and said, "No mom. I AM happy."

I could not help but reflect on the radical change. Changed words and changed actions. He had the pen and was writing his story.

Faith. Respected. Appreciated. Victorious. Transformed. Happy. Loved.
Now those are words worth a replay.

"Live life as if everything is rigged in your favor."
RUMI

The Power of Positivity

There is no doubt that the voice we hear in our head is the combination of many experiences and underlying beliefs. That does not change the fact that we can choose the words that voice uses and thereby change the affect the voice has on us. Often, this is where the victim versus victor mentality or negativity versus positivity comes into play.

Martin E.P. Seligman is widely considered to be the father of positive psychology. He has written many books and *Learned Optimism: How to Change Your Mind and Your Life* offers insight that is congruent with my assertion that the voice in your head is a choice. Through his ongoing projects at the University of Pennsylvania, Seligman has improved our understanding of self-esteem and the value of learned optimism. Seligman outlines the downside of the self-esteem movement that began in California in the 1960s. He provides an overview of the detrimental effects that teaching self-esteem might have in the United States. In the last 10 years, the literature suggests that teaching self-esteem is not the anecdote to depression or negativity. In fact, studies indicate that children with high self-esteem, when confronted with real world challenges, turn to aggression and violence. He reported that after extensive investigation, he found no evidence of causality of improved self-esteem and doing well at work, in school, and with the people you love. He asserts, "Self-esteem seems only to be a symptom, a correlate, of how well a person is doing in the world." (Seligman, 2006)

Seligman's focus has been how to improve optimism, which has proven to prevent depression and related symptoms. I highly recommend his book for a deeper look into the effects of optimism on depression, achievement, sports, children, and school. I particularly like his exercise on identifying the ABCs – adversity, belief, and consequences – of things that happen in your daily life. These exercises drive home the value of contemplating how you think, which in turn drives the voice in your head. He easily illustrates the connection between the ways you think about adversity and how that makes you feel and potentially act. He provides concrete examples on how to manage your "negative dialogue." His comment that, "One of the most significant findings in psychology in the past 20 years is that individuals can choose the way they think," fully supports the necessity for us to consider the words we choose for the voice in our heads.

Another important book came out in 2020, Kimberly Faith's *Your Lion Inside: Discover the Power Within and Live Your Fullest Life*. Her work is complementary to Seligman's and takes a more specific look at the challenges women face. Her main message is that the time is now for women to break the glass ceilings in their worlds by first using them as mirrors and by changing the narrative. She introduces seven sisters of the sisterhood who each provide their mental model stages of awareness, choice, and freedom. Her seven sisters do a fantastic job showing the progression through the three mental model stages. These mental models equate to what I have been calling the voice in your head, which indeed is your narrative (Faith, 2020).

Taking a closer look at how a child processes information is helpful. How does the voice in her head develop? It reflects what she hears. As we become adults, we can choose to hold on to those same words and therefore our beliefs in what the words are saying to us, or we can change the story. Accepting the story formed by the words in your head is your choice and your choice only. Additionally, only you can change the story, which begins by reflecting on the words you currently choose.

Let us work through a simple example.

ACTIVITY

Fill in the following blanks:

1. This weekend I have to _____

2. This weekend I should _____

I would assume that at least some of the readers answer "do the laundry" or "clean the house." We will select "do the laundry" to further explore, but you can apply this exercise to whatever you answered.

Fill in the following:

1. The value in doing the laundry is...

2. And the value in that is...

3. How does this action (doing the laundry) get accomplished?

4. Is this action something I am grateful for? Why?

5. Based on this knowledge, how might I reframe what I will do this weekend?

Potential Answers:

1. Clean clothes.

2. I enjoy having my clothes clean.

3. By using hot water in my washing machine.

4. Yes, because it would be much harder to have clean clothes without water and a washer (and dryer).

5. I want to do the laundry this weekend OR I get to do the laundry this weekend OR I am able to do the laundry this weekend.

This brings us to gratitude. People who maintain a positive outlook typically come from a place of strong gratitude, most of the time. Some people profess to be grateful for all they have. Yet, these same people listen to a voice that tells them what they "have" to or "should" do and they fail to recognize truly being grateful can change the story they find themselves in. Another way to contemplate this is to consider, "What's the alternative?"

In my example above, what is the alternative to doing the laundry on the weekend? I would not have clean clothes. The alternative of not being able to do the laundry on the weekend might be that I'm not healthy enough to do so or that I lack the proper resources such as clean water, a washing machine, even detergent. But if I have all these things then I can change the voice in my head to reflect how positive the situation is and how grateful I am. This might sound like, "I get to do the laundry this weekend" or "I'm able to do the laundry this weekend" or "I'm going to do the laundry this weekend." None of these statements reflect an imposition or a lack of gratitude for the resources I have. Nor do they reflect that I am doing the laundry out of any obligation.

If I was doing the laundry for someone else and the voice said, "I have to do the laundry for Mrs. Rank this weekend," I would need to contemplate whether this obligation was something that I chose. Is it an opportunity that I am grateful for or one born out of my value of kindness? If so, the only obligation I have is to honor that value. The voice might say, "I'm grateful to fulfill the kindness I wanted to show Mrs. Rank."

The voice is a choice. There are two choices. The first is whether to believe the voice. Is what you hear and the word choices representative of your values, beliefs, and your intent? Is what the voice says of true value to you? You may decide the voice is on point and only requires the refinement of some of your extensively used words. The second choice is how to change the voice. If you have concluded that the voice in your head does not align with your values, then your next step would be a commitment to changing the words you allow to be heard. The degree of difficulty in doing this varies from person to person, as does the desire.

There are many opportunities for working towards making better choices with the words in your head. Some of them include finding a good coach, allowing time and space for self-reflection, even attending a mindfulness retreat. Using words that are more consistently positive, grateful, and reflective of your values supports any work you may get to do in altering the words you use with others.

Stifle the Shoulds

Often people ask me how I ended up in California and my response is, "because of the 'shoulds'." I grew up in Maryland where abiding by Emily Post-type manners and rules of civility was an expectation. Not all of you will recall that Emily Post was the go-to authority for manners and social standards. This included the rules around weddings, parties, and even the types of clothing, shoes, and purses that were appropriate at certain times of the year. No doubt you have heard, "You don't wear white after Labor Day." Ms. Post wrote the original book on the words to choose for invitations, RSVPs, and correspondence. She directed what was socially correct well before politically correct became a thing. The people I met in my early twenties while living in San Francisco seemed to know nothing of these alleged rules. This led me to believe what I "should" do is stay.

This brings us back to values and bias. When I was firmly rooted in a society that abided by such rules, I was apt to judge others when they breached them. I developed an inherent bias towards what I understood to be socially correct. I chose words that supported this alleged correctness. This included speaking in terms of what one shouldn't, or can't, or mustn't do. As I became more in touch with my personal values, I realized how misaligned I was with these alleged rules. I abandoned them. As you might imagine, such beliefs can be very deeply rooted. Occasionally, I still hear the voice in my head question my choice to wear an open-toed shoe in winter.

Now when I hear someone suggest that I "should" do something, I have trained the voice in my head, as well as my actual voice, to ask why. When I hear the voice in my head suggest judgment, based on an old bias, I ask why. I also ask, "What purpose does this serve?" This enables clarity that I "should" only do those things that align with my values.

I like to repeat: I choose my values, I set my intentions, I choose the words I hear in my head (my story), I choose the words I speak. I invite you to consider these commitments as well as: I choose to do the work to improve my Emotional Intelligence, which will positively influence my self-esteem. Here is a story of how this has worked out for someone else and the impact of the words of another.

The Words Others Choose

STORY — HOW WORDS AFFECTED SARAH HENRY

When I was looking for a story related to the impact of the words others choose for us, Sarah Margaret Henry's story appeared in my Facebook feed. Exactly what appeared is provided below with Sarah's permission. When I met Sarah, I learned that she is the owner of Still Poetry Photography, a multimedia production company. She is an author, photographer, filmmaker and she operates a YouTube channel. She writes passionately about all sorts of important topics, including women's rights and animal adoption. She uses her voice to tell underprivileged stories; stories we may not want to talk about. She makes them larger and more beautiful in order to give access to those who aren't living their true lives and to validate those who are. Although she was told that studying the arts and humanities would lead her nowhere, she has most certainly utilized her experiences and her education. In her book, *Intricacies Are Just Cracks in The Wall* (Henry, 2019), she uses her voice beautifully to advocate for others and make this world a better place. She exemplifies the power of words!

Sarah's Post — including her poem

In elementary school when grownups asked me what I wanted to be when I grew up, I said, "I'm gonna be an author! Just like J.K. Rowling!"

Not "I want to be an author."

I am going to be an author.

Most people said, "Aw, that's cute!" They tousled my hair, maybe pinched my cheeks.

I wrote constantly. There are journals and notebooks and scraps of paper throughout my parent's house of my writing from kindergarten up through high school, and my apartment now is covered with even more notebooks I've filled to the brim with thoughts, characters, poems, the dreams I cannot wake up from.

In high school, when people started asking what I was planning on pursuing in college, I said, "I'm double majoring in English and Communications."

No one tousled my hair.

I got, "Good luck with that. Hope you enjoy being unemployed. Sounds like a good major for a future housewife."

I didn't even dare tell them, "I'm going to be an author."

I didn't want them to laugh in my face.

I wasted a year and a half of my life with someone who told me that because he was pursuing a degree in science, it was more important than whatever degree I could get.

I struggled with depression, anxiety, bi-polar disorder since I was eight: Things he told me were my fault and that I should just get over.

When he sexually assaulted me repeatedly, I added PTSD to the list.

I didn't seek medical help until I was 19.

I left him.

I started writing again.

I wrote the tears, the blood, the pains, the demons latched onto my spine. I wrote my heart away and bound it in a book, for any and all to see. I no longer care what people think of me.

And now I'm an author.

Just like I always told them I would be.

The final page of INTRICACIES ARE JUST CRACKS IN THE WALL:
I am
I want the light in my eyes
to be contagious, want the
sinew in my thighs to evoke
another's self-forgiveness.

I want my toes to teach
her that it was never a sin
to dance. I want my neck to
be held high enough to be a beacon,
I want my ears to believe that
listening is life changing. I want
my heart to be an organ
that belongs to itself, not donated
at another's discretion. I want
my fire to burn roses because
I am a gift unto myself.

"Sticks and stones may break my bones, but words will never harm me." Ah, but they may. They may keep you from realizing your full potential. They may keep you from being true to yourself and your values. They may inhibit your creativity or growth. They may impact your relationships. They may influence how you converse with others. Whether you hear such words spoken to you by another or as the voice in your head, they will affect your sense of self.

There are words that harm when heard as the voice in your head. There are words and phrases that cast doubt such as *can't, shouldn't, won't be able to, not capable,* or simply *no.* When we reflect on something, an action or intent, and the voice says "no," doubt has been introduced. Negativity is offered in place of positivity and confidence. Curiosity is stifled. Can you recall an example in your life?

REFLECTION

1. What thought do you have that occasionally gets met with a negative thought, such as *no, not likely, don't think so, unlikely,* or *can't?*

2. What does that negative assignment (word choice) to the thought bring up for you?

3. What do you believe about the word choice?

4.   What effect do your beliefs have on your actions?

5.   How might you change the word choice?

Self-Love

So many things impact self-love. So far, we have covered Emotional Intelligence, self-esteem, the voice in your head, judgment from others, judgment of yourself, and inherent biases. Most importantly, we have explored choice. It is your choice to further improve your Emotional Intelligence, which is reflected in your self-esteem. It is your choice to show up as a witness to your life and those around you, and not in judgment. Positivity is your choice. Owning the words in your head, as well as the ones that come out of your mouth, is your choice. Each of these choices impacts your self-love. Choose wisely.

Just – A Form of Self-Sabotage

I have always appreciated the story of when President Kennedy visited NASA in 1961. He happened upon a janitor who was mopping a floor. He introduced himself and asked the janitor what he did for NASA. It may strike you that his answer would have been obvious to our esteemed leader. For 58 years, many people have shared his answer. It represents the impact our words have when they support our intention. He said, "I'm helping to put a man on the moon." This janitor's words impart that his contribution was of value and that he was a part of something greater. Leaders use this example routinely to connect how important it is for employees to be engaged in the vision and mission of an organization.

A more common response may have been, "I'm just the janitor." Or "I just keep things clean around here." The operative word choice here is "just." As an adjective *just* typically means lawful, proper, fair, or righteous. As an adverb, it typically means exactly, precisely, or barely, only, simply. When we use *just* as a description of ourselves or related to our actions or contributions, it is these last three words that come to mind. This denigrates our intention and serves no purpose.

📖 STORY: WHAT "JUST A" SAYS

I was once visiting a patient when a dietitian entered the room. She had what looked like a lab coat on, as did many of the other people who entered that room. This patient was older, medicated, and having difficulty keeping things straight. The dietitian was double-checking the lunch order. When the patient asked who she was, she responded, "I'm just the dietitian." She may have been thinking about her role in comparison to that of the nurse or the physician and signaling that she would not be causing any pain or doing anything complicated. She may have been thinking of her long-term career plans. She may have even been thinking of how her role fits into that of the entire organization. Either way, she missed several opportunities.

1. She missed an opportunity to connect what she does daily to the mission of the organization.
2. She missed an opportunity to impart to the patient the skills she brings to the patient's care.
3. She missed an opportunity to support herself and enhance her inner voice.
4. She missed an opportunity to connect to her values and intent.

Here are some suggestions she might consider for greater impact:

- I am a registered dietitian, which means I am responsible for your nutrition.
- I am a registered dietitian on our fantastic culinary team.
- I am a registered dietitian and excited about my role in your care. I ensure we meet your dietary needs.

In the section on managing up (Chapter Four), the focus is on how the choice of words affects the listener. The choice also affects the speaker. Saying over time that you are just a _____ diminishes the value of your role, as well as your perception of yourself. *Just* as a qualifier signals a lack of confidence and low self-esteem.

If you listen closely, you will hear the use of the word "just" quite often. It is commonly used as a qualifier when giving instructions or providing information. And it is unnecessary.

REFLECTION

Reflect on the difference between the two expressions below. Which of the following words might you choose to represent how the statement made you feel?

Unsure, confident, undecided, aligned, uncertain, certain, clear, ambiguous...add your own words.

Which is better, the first sentence or the second sentence below? Why is it better? How has the impact changed? What feeling would you assign?

1.   I am just going to show you how the results support our progress.
2.   I would like to show you how the results support our progress.

1.   I just want to provide you with some examples.
2.   Here are some examples.

1.   I just have to decide what to do next. (*Just* AND *have to*)
2.   I will decide what to do next.

1.   I am just one of the people you will speak with.
2.   I am one of several people you will speak with.

Choosing to eliminate the word *just* reframes the sentiment to one of sufficiency. In this same sense, I suggest the word *enough* be used sparingly when referring to one's self. I have heard women use this word in support of another woman, even using it as encouragement. For example, "You are good enough" or "You have to tell yourself you have done enough." I propose this word is *not* enough. Indeed there are more affirmative ways to support yourself or your actions. Replace *enough* with *perfect, fantastic, exactly right, spot on,* or any word choice that does not minimize you or your effort.

> "Speak when you are angry and you will make the best speech you'll ever regret."
>
> AMBROSE BIERCE

Sarcasm and Defensiveness

I come from a lineage of sarcasm and married into another one. There is no doubt that sarcasm can provide humor, which is at its best when no one is a victim. However, this is rarely the case. The victim can be you (the speaker), your psyche (inner voice), someone spoken about, or someone spoken to – there are a plethora of potential victims. In my experience, sarcasm appears tied to defensiveness. A sarcastic response (choice of words) is often provided from a place of defensiveness. And other than humor, there is no value provided. The value of the humor must be extraordinarily strong to warrant the risk of utilizing sarcasm with your word choices. Sometimes, the humor presents as self-depreciating.

Think of it as a large popcorn at the theater. It is very satisfying for a while, until it is not. In this case, the self-depreciation may be endearing to your audience, but it takes its toll on your self-worth. This is true when you believe the words you choose to be true and not the case if you know them to be untrue.

Defensive responses can seem automatic for some people. The interesting thing about defensiveness is that it is often so obvious. I wonder why the speaker does not also realize the defensiveness in his words. This typically strikes me when someone leads with something he does not hold to be true. For example, "I don't really care about that," "that won't bother me," "it wasn't my fault." I am not saying that in all cases the speaker will not believe these statements to be true, but often after deep consideration, this is not the case. What he is asserting establishes his potential defensiveness.

Here is an example that involves word choices. Suppose someone chooses a word that is either grammatically incorrect or its meaning does not apply to what she is trying to convey. If she is questioned for clarity and responds, "You know what I mean!" she is being defensive. She is not owning her mistake and instead is placing blame on the other person.

How can you prevent being defensive? Start with good self-awareness. When in a conversation, if you hear something that does not align with your values and potentially causes you conflict, pause and think about your response. If during your pause you suspect any defensive thoughts, consider owning them. This might play out with you saying, "I need to think about that. What you are suggesting conflicts with my values and it makes me want to defend them." Or "I'm having a defensive reaction to what you just shared and I'd like some time to think about this before I respond."

When you are the receiver of a defensive response, also pause. Contemplate what you just said and why it may have triggered the defense mechanisms of the other person. Then ask for clarification in a safe, non-judgmental way. This is the tricky part because your words have the potential of causing even more defensiveness. Ironically, I have rarely seen a person who is called out for being defensive not defend her position. Therefore, your first consideration before you bring your observation to her might be, "What purpose will this serve?" If her defensiveness will hold up whatever is being discussed (in other words, you do not truly have her buy in) or is perceived to be part of a larger issue or is a recurring pattern that you feel compelled to address, then you need to proceed and choose your words wisely. Here are some suggestions:

1. Your response surprises/confuses/interests me. May I ask you some questions to better understand your position?

2. Your response (perhaps body language) makes me think we should dig a little deeper into this topic. What are you feeling about this? What did this bring up for you?
3. What additional information can I provide?
4. How was your response related to your values? I would like to understand more fully.

Chapter Wrap

I always want to use my voice for the good of all. I value courage and self-exploration. I consciously guided my internal voice toward a narrative that is supportive of my values and this led to the creation of this book. I hope that what I have written expands your courage and self-exploration as well. The exercises proposed will help you look at your words in a different light. Be true to them. Do not allow the words of others to overshadow your truth. Be specific with the voice in your head and connect it to what is in your heart.

Conversations with loved ones can pose individual and recurring challenges. Dissecting certain patterns and triggers can help establish boundaries. You can learn to respond differently. Adhering to your values will support word choices with loved ones. Let us take a deeper look at how to do so.

> "A smart person knows what to say, a wise person knows whether or not to say it."
>
> UNKNOWN

Chapter TWO

WORDS THAT CONNECT WITH LOVED ONES

Patterns Impact our Words

At the end of my yoga class in early January, my instructor shared that an interaction over the holidays had prompted her to set the intention of always coming from her heart when communicating. Surreina very graciously shared with me the following story.

STORY: WORDS TANGLED UP IN LOVE

On Christmas Day, Surreina and her husband were heading off to see her family. She alluded to the importance of this context in setting the stage for the exchange that occurred based on a minor car issue. The key fob to her car does not operate properly and only unlocks the driver's door. This has been going on for quite some time and every time she travels with her husband, he must wait until she gets in the car to open his side. This delay frequently causes him to comment and express frustration.

This day was no different and her husband expressed his annoyance at the delay. Surreina immediately responded from a place of irritation, "How many times do you have to do that until you learn?" (Meaning, attempt to unlock the passenger door before she gets in and does it manually).

Adam snapped back, "When you love somebody you open the door for them." Surreina was immediately hurt and could not believe he was questioning her love. She could not imagine how the few seconds dealing with the broken door lock would lead to such a comment. Adam added, "Darren (his buddy) does that too, but I expect it from him." (Meaning, Darren makes him wait.)

By this point, Surreina was quite ruffled. She responded, "It seems you have been in a bad place all morning and you need to figure out why that is, and don't take it out on me." After several moments of pushing him for an admission of guilt and a verbal volley back and forth, Surreina knew she had to step back. She paused to assess her feelings and decided she needed to own them. Her next response was, "You're right; I was not being very patient. I should not have snapped at you."

As Surreina contemplated the situation, she realized she had neglected to insert compassion and had made the focus on Adam and not what she was feeling. She went on to apologize and let him know she initially missed the cues of his irritability and that his reaction had hurt her feelings. She shared that they both softened and realized that it was "just words" that had caused the upset. When Surreina chose to own her response, she came back to the conversation in a more cognizant emotional state. The apology was genuine and she assured Adam that she felt his love.

Surreina has set the intention to get to the softer place sooner or prevent the irritation from occurring altogether. Shortly after this incident, she shared what happened with a friend. The friend commented, "I've always admired how much you speak from your heart." Surreina realized that although this may typically be the case, she wishes to cultivate a heart-centered life with everyone. She desires to show up with patience and compassion with her loved ones. She shared that past patterns can create triggers with both her husband and mother. Surreina's intention is to practice pausing to fully reflect on how to say what she wishes with emotional sincerity. This includes leading with "I" statements. It also means considering the timing for the other person, as well as her own sense of presence, before she speaks.

Surreina's story reminds me of two adages: *You can choose your friends but not your family* and *You cannot unsay anything*. These two adages have always given me pause when a substantive family conversation occurs. A pause is exactly what you need as it allows for time to reflect on your values and your intention. "Loved ones" covers a broad range of personal connections. My intention is not to exclude anyone, but to offer an overview of some general scenarios relevant to immediate family members and significant others.

As Surreina realized, patterns often govern how we respond to situations, especially recurring ones. We have these patterns with our parents, siblings, spouses, and significant others. If the pattern you find yourself in does not serve your values, it is time to change the pattern. First, you need to recognize and own your part in the pattern. Triggers and repetitive behaviors drive patterns. These can be complicated and practiced for decades. This does not make them right or aligned with who you are and how you wish to express yourself. Your pattern might be the reflection of another's response or behavior. All of this is worthy of consideration and may warrant a qualified coach. A good coach will know if and when to direct you to a session with a clinical therapist.

How do you know if it is time to seek help? Here are some points to consider:

- Do you find yourself in the same non-productive conversation with a loved one?
- Do you work to change the narrative, only to end up in the same uncomfortable place – one that does not truly represent you?
- Do you feel the words you choose aren't truly heard and trigger predictable responses?
- Does a visit with a loved one feel like Groundhog Day?
- Do confrontations always end with your concession?
- Are you apprehensive to say what you really mean?
- Do you repress your feelings and needs so you do not upset or trigger a loved one?

You gain clarity the more you own your words and consistently choose ones that align with your values and purpose. You can practice the following techniques and decide which of these steps could improve upon any growth limiting familial patterns you are choosing to hold.

1. **Own your message** – Regardless of how ingrained patterns are, at some point you must take responsibility for your words. Careful consideration of your words, ones that support your intent, is paramount. This means you must own your intention. Is your intention for the greater good of all? Is it only self-serving? Will it cause injury to another? If so, is that necessary?

2. **Speak in terms of "I"** – When in a challenging conversation, it is especially important to stick to expressing what you own, feel, or know. Resist the urge to speak in terms of "you" – when referring to what the other person did or said. As an example, it is best to say, "When we argue like this, **I** seldom feel heard." As opposed to, "**You** never listen to me."

3. **Lean into your values** – If you value honesty, integrity, and family, contemplate the outcome of your words on these values. Will your honesty impede your ability to communicate with your family as you would like? Which values serve your intentions the best? How will you balance them?

4. **Listen really, really well** – Is it possible that after many years of patterns, you anticipate or assume a response? How does this affect your words? Once you change your approach to better represent you, pause and listen for the potential change in a response pattern.

5. **Assess your responses and triggers** – What triggers you? How do familial patterns affect your word choices? Do you have a certain posture or routine approach that is not emblematic of your true intention? Do you always come from a place of love, acceptance, and understanding?

6. **Build a better pattern** – Rome was not built in a day. If you have relationship patterns that you would like to change to

reach a greater connection with a loved one, you need to commit to working toward a better pattern. You need to reach for communication founded on your values, intention, and love.

Connect with Children

One of the first words a child learns is "no." And it's often expressed with an exclamation point. They will parrot whatever they hear. They will most certainly learn bias through the words they hear. This may be the most important time to consider the words you choose.

While there are many books on the topic of raising children, two stand out for advising on communication. My favorite when our children were young was *Reviving Ophelia: Saving the Selves of Adolescent Girls* by Mary Pipher PhD. In 2019, the 25th Anniversary Edition was published and included a video and related materials. More recently, Jim Taylor's work in *Your Children are Listening: Nine Messages They Need to Hear from You* has gained traction. Published in 2011, Taylor's book outlines nine positive messages that are important for parents to impart to their children. His book overviews not just the words, but the emotions and actions that are part of a parent's messaging to a child. (Gilliam, M. P., 2019) (Taylor, 2011)

Psychotherapist Mary Pipher originally published *Reviving Ophelia* in 1994. In 2019, she and her daughter Sarah Pipher Gilliam updated the book based on current trends, including the use of cell phones and social media. This 25th anniversary edition focuses on the issues that face 21st century teenage girls. They tackle why girls struggle with misogyny, sexism, and issues of identity and self-esteem. As you might imagine, much of this is related to the words that are used in their presence. Just as Pipher did in the original book, she provides mini case studies, as well as recommendations for parents, teachers, and counselors. These recommendations set the foundational understanding of the prevalent issues that the book explores. The next step is for teachers, parents, and counselors to choose the right words when they interact with adolescent girls. (Gilliam, M. P., 2019)

Nature AND Nurture

While the parents, or their genes, are responsible for the nature part of the development equation, we are all responsible for the nurture part. "It takes a village" is an understatement. Kids soak up the world by observing and listening to everything and everyone. They hear how we speak to others, whether we are on the phone, at dinner, or in public places. They file the words we choose for use later. When they say their first swear words, the only shock should be, "Why did I not think they were listening?"

Let us explore some scenarios of what a child may hear. Persistently hearing "no" teaches them that when they do certain things, they will get a response from their parents. This response is predictable and recurrent. It becomes something they can control. The response of "no" is sometimes born out of safety and without any consideration for the impact. Offering "no" repeatedly to a child results in diminishing the impact. The alternative is to change the situation to one that is acceptable. For example, if a child is reaching for your best china, offer her something else instead. Redirecting is the same as reframing something from negative to positive.

In addition to the use of "no" is the use of terms and phrases such as "you can't," "don't," and "please stop," in a negative vein. Positive psychology experts teach us that the most effective way to have acceptable behaviors repeated is to reinforce them. It takes much more conscious effort to focus on the positive and continually reinforce appropriate behavior. Even saying "good boy" or "good girl" has a different impact than choosing words that reinforce a behavior.

Positive reinforcement involves being specific about the behavior you observe and would like repeated. Using "good" as the qualifier for a child does not reinforce any specific behavior. Assign "good" to the action. For example, "You did a good job tidying up your room." Saying "good boy" as reinforcement for tidying a room, does not have the same impact.

Leading with what a child *can* do is impactful at the earliest age all the way through the teen years. When they are infants and toddlers, this may look more like you showing them what they *can do* or *can have* to play with. As they get older this thought process bears out in discussions. As a reminder from Chapter One, leading with "why" is incredibly important.

As a child grows, he invariably makes decisions that conflict with family values. How parents respond, including the words they choose, may have a lasting impact. Kids of all ages are adept at asking "why?" and "because I said so" has never been an effective response. In Chapter One we began with an exploration of core values. Expressing the "why" behind a decision or an outcome requires an understanding of shared values. Discussing shared values with a child throughout his childhood makes conversations regarding choices and consequences much easier.

STORY: SIBLING HITTING

Most parents have dealt with a child who bites or hits another. When our daughter was 18 months old and our son was approaching three, our son whacked our daughter. As this was a little more than 20 years ago, I provide an overview of my recollection. There is no doubt that it did not play out as perfectly as I describe. Suffice it to say that after many years of learning and self-awareness, this is how I would have wanted it to go.

Erik wielded an aluminum tube. I caught the act out of the corner of my eye. There was no mistaking that he swung the aluminum tube with the intent of hitting Taylor in the head. His target wailed. These are the times when emotions, such as anger and sadness, cloud our ability to choose words wisely. Yelling "no!" or anything from my place of anger would serve no purpose. I separated the two of them, putting Erik in a bedroom. I consoled Taylor and assessed any damage to her precious head. I settled Taylor in the care of her aunt.

As I returned to Erik, I took several deep breaths and centered myself. I struggled to find the calm I needed to make the most of this teachable moment. When I entered the room, he was crying as well. I was unsure if this was out of remorse or anticipation of my reaction. I knelt in front of him as he sat on the bed and looked deep into his eyes. I invited him to take a deep breath with me. I held his tiny hands and began to explain the impact of what he had done. I wanted to ask him, "What were you thinking?" and "Why did you do that?" I suspect at 3 years old, he was operating on sheer impulse. I explained to him how badly he had hurt his sister. I told him that she loved him and I loved him, and that I was sure he loved her. I said it was important for us to always be kind to each other and that being kind meant not harming each other. He told me that she had taken one of his toys. I validated his feelings of anger and reiterated that regardless of how we felt, we would not harm one another. I asked him how he would feel if I or his sister hit him on the head. After our discussion, we left the room to return to his sister so he could apologize.

I have a truly clear recollection that it was always harder to take the time to do the right thing. Reacting, giving in, or simply not addressing an issue always seems easier. If the first step is choosing to be present and respond, then the second step is how you will respond. This requires contemplation of the most impactful word choices.

The Inadvertent Seeds of Gender Bias

I learned by reading *Reviving Ophelia* of the impact our perceptions of gender can have. They provide conditioning and therefore biases of which we are unaware. For example, when driving in my minivan with two toddlers and seeing a large backhoe in the distance, I am apt to say, "Look at that guy digging that big ditch." Or worse I may have led with "Erik, look at that guy digging that big ditch." When I inadvertently make such comments repeatedly, I am teaching my children that only boys align with heavy equipment use and such jobs.

I have done this by speaking directly to my son while my daughter is present, as well as by assuming the ditch digger was a man. This may seem minor, but over the course of several years the impact grows.

What words might I choose differently? To start, I would not single out my son for such an observation, or my daughter for an observation that is typically feminine. I will involve them equally in observations and commentary. Secondly, I will consider my use of pronouns as well as gender assignment when pointing something out to my children. For example, if I am telling a story that involves a physician I may say "she." At the very least, I will commit to a healthy balance of masculine and feminine pronouns when gender is unknown. I will also purposely choose the opposite pronoun for discussions on jobs typically perceived as gender specific.

There are developmental stages of our children that we celebrate and there are those that we fear. Baby's first word, baby's first step, baby rolling over, baby's first sentence are all stages that we celebrate. Isolated in the bedroom, difficult to converse with, moody due to hormones, and apathetic when asked questions are developmental stages we may fear. Just as our words matter when we pass celebratory stages, they are especially important during the challenging stages. During this time, it is better to be inquisitive and curious without judgment. This requires more asking and less telling. Every conversation has the potential to either build upon or denigrate self-esteem.

Spark Dialogue – Powerful Questions

Here are some impactful questions for consideration. Leading with "what," "how," or "tell me..." leads to more open-ended dialogue. Unless you desire a monosyllabic response, stay clear of "yes" or "no" questions. With teens, asking questions about feelings that begin with "how" can also lead to concise answers. The most common example of this is, "How was school today?" and the response, "Fine."

The following are a few ways to reframe the question to engage more dialogue with your children:

1. What was the best part of school today? Why?
2. What happened at school today that made you laugh?
3. What was the worst thing that happened today?
4. What was the funniest thing you did today?
5. What would you change about today?
6. What did you do today that may have made someone happy?
7. Tell me the most interesting thing you learned today.
8. How did you show your true self today?
9. Tell me about something one of your friends did that affected you today.
10. Tell me what made today special.

You can modify the same questions for conversations at the dinner table, in the car, in the bedroom doorway and to be specific to an event other than school. Step one is asking questions that are more engaging. Step two is to refrain from judgment. This brings us to choosing the right words when you respond.

Our children perceive that we are judging them before we even open our mouths. This is even more reason why we must choose our responses carefully.

REFLECTION

Review the responses in column three. Circle any words that may imply judgment or simply not align with intent. In the last column, review the reframed response.

Question	Child's Answer	Parent Response	Better Response/ Words
What was the worst thing that happened today?	My lunch was the worst thing about today. I can't believe you thought I would eat a mushy sandwich like that.	I did not make you a mushy sandwich. How did it get that way? Where did you keep it?	Honey, I'm so sorry to hear it was mushy. It was certainly not my intent. Let's have a look at what will work better for you tomorrow. Thanks for telling me.
What would you change about today?	Nothing.	Really? Everything was just so perfect? Are you being honest?	Wow, that's great. Tell me the best parts.
Tell me about something one of your friends did that affected you today.	Alicia sat in my usual seat at lunchtime.	Well that doesn't sound so bad. I'm sure there are plenty of other seats.	Tell me more about that. How did it affect you?

ACTIVITY

List the last two things you heard from a child or young adult in column one. In column two, write your best response. Reflect on the words you chose. Did they serve your purpose? Were they non-judgmental?

Last thing I heard a kid/young adult say:	My response:

Let us revisit the 5:1 ratio for positive to negative feedback mentioned in Chapter One. Even when children do something that conflicts with family values, there is still something positive to reinforce. Maintaining a healthy ratio of positive reinforcement builds up credibility for being objective when there is a difficult situation. Said differently, the recipients have perceived balanced acknowledgment of what they do well and may be more open when an uncomfortable discussion arises.

Receiving a barrage of negative input can be as detrimental as receiving no input at all. Others may perceive no input as lack of caring, lack of understanding, lack of knowledge, or disagreement. Regarding any negative response, the first consideration should be, "Does this feedback serve any purpose?"

STORY: POSITIVE REINFORCEMENT PAY OFF

When our son was a senior in high school, he went to a stranger's house to look at some skis advertised on Craigslist. The man invited him and his buddy into his house to smoke some pot. They accepted and he called us a while later after realizing he was too high to drive home. I believe he decided to call us based on how we had consistently reinforced his good decisions. He was able to decide on his own that he had made a bad choice. Once he was home safely, our discussion revolved around how he got himself in that situation and what he may have done differently or would do differently in the future. We provided positive reinforcement for the courage it took for him to know he should not drive and that he could call us.

> "Life has a way of talking to the future. It's called memory."
> RICHARD POWERS.

The Competence Conundrum

Most adults I know will tell you that when they are around their families, particularly their parents, they are treated as children. Oftentimes I hear people say, "I'm 12 years old again." It has always fascinated me that an elder who was quite competent in his or her 50s, does not assume the same competence when his or her children or other adults around them reach that same age. You might hear, "I will always be your mother" or "I'm your father." That does not negate the experience children gain over many years. Honoring that experience should be a simple thing. It is not necessary for there to be any competition or association of roles at this point. Adult children may have children of their own and may have incredible life experiences. It serves no purpose for the parent to denigrate adult children with the words he or she chooses. This is often exhibited in words chosen to critique small things such as cooking, cleaning, or driving. Perhaps it is a reflection of the elder's waning experience in these areas.

I am convinced that it is not the intention of the parent to make the child feel inadequate. It may be that a mother simply cannot help herself from being instructive even when it is no longer needed. Adult children have opportunities to correct their own parenting mistakes – ones their parents may have also made. For example, as the last word during punishment, one child often heard his mother yell in frustration, "I hope someday you have a child just like you! Then you'll understand what you put us through." When he became a dad, he reframed her statement. "I hope someday you will have a child as wonderful as you."

Active Listening

Sometimes the best words to choose are no words at all. Previously, we reviewed when words serve no purpose. We have also reviewed the value of asking more powerful questions, such as ones that begin with the words "what," or "how," or "tell me." When we listen well to responses, we hear even what is not said. Active listening requires being fully present in the dialogue.

This is quite a challenge in today's world with technology bombardment. The inability to listen well sets one up for miscommunication and misunderstanding. Some active listening tips include:

1. Be Present – Where is your mind? Think about the person with whom you are conversing and really be there. Seek to hear his words and understand him.

2. Avoid Distractions – Do not look at your phone. Do not text or email or check social media. Do not type while on a call. See No. 1.

3. Consider Word Choice – Choose appropriate words and phrases to use such as – "I hear you." "I am listening." "I want to fully understand." "Do you mind if I ask clarifying questions?"

4. Demonstrate you are listening well through actions and words – Periodically paraphrase what you hear. Look the speaker in the eye. Lean in. Provide verbal affirmations such as "I see," "I understand," and "Yes."

5. Do not interrupt – Interrupting is a sure sign you are not

actively listening. You are jumping ahead and not giving the speaker the space to choose her words wisely.

Advice

A wise mother of five daughters once told me, "I never give advice, unless asked for it. Even then I proceed with caution." When you are inclined to offer advice, consider this flow chart:

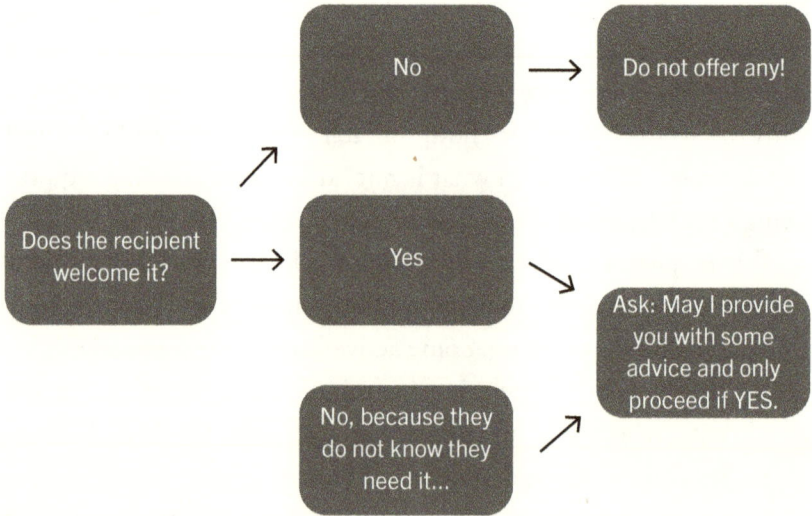

```
                        ┌──────────┐        ┌─────────────────┐
                        │   No     │  ──▶   │ Do not offer any!│
                        └──────────┘        └─────────────────┘
                             ↗
┌─────────────────┐        ┌──────────┐
│ Does the recipient│ ──▶  │   Yes    │ ↘
│  welcome it?     │        └──────────┘     ┌─────────────────┐
└─────────────────┘                          │ Ask: May I provide│
                                             │  you with some   │
                        ┌──────────────┐     │  advice and only │
                        │ No, because they│   │  proceed if YES. │
                        │ do not know they│ ↗ └─────────────────┘
                        │   need it...    │
                        └──────────────┘
```

Chapter Wrap

I recently visited a friend who asked me to pull a bin out of her closet. The bin was marked "inherited linens" and it held the most exquisite lace and embroidered works. It also housed the most remarkable quilt I have ever seen. We spoke about the efforts of her female ancestors to create such beauty. We imagined a group of women working endlessly on the quilt that was made of 1-inch hexagons in various fabrics and patterns and fit a full-size bed. All of it was hand sewn. I have since contemplated the fact that so much of our ancestry is woven into the fabric of our daily lives. You cannot simply shake the wrinkles from your past and the patterns that have been created.

When it comes to relating to loved ones, it may be more challenging to lead with your values. Carefully crafted patterns that have survived decades are worth exploration if you desire to communicate better. If you allow your heart to inform your intention in any conversation, you will choose words that truly represent you. You get to decide who you surround yourself with. Hopefully, you choose those who provide you with a fresh respective and help you advance your contribution to the world. The more we relate to others who are unlike us, the more we learn.

"Compassion impels us to work tirelessly to alleviate the suffering of our fellow creatures, to dethrone ourselves from the centre of our world and put another there, and to honour the inviolable sanctity of every single human being, treating everybody, without exception, with absolute justice, equity and respect."

KAREN ARMSTRONG

Chapter THREE

WORDS THAT CONNECT WITH OTHERS

PART ONE: COMMON ENCOUNTERS

Debate, Dialogue and Devil's Advocate

We were thrilled when our son joined the debate team in high school. During his time at Loyola Sacred Heart (LSH) in Missoula, Montana, the debate team held the record for the winningest high school team of all time. They had won 30 state championships. More importantly, he learned the art of a good debate. He learned to choose his words for impact and to base them on well-researched facts. Ultimately, the art of debate affirms that all the preparation in the world is meaningless if words are not conveyed properly.

I recall the portable plastic file boxes the kids stockpiled with information in case they needed source material to document their arguments. They worked for weeks to fill their containers and minds with knowledge, statistics, and specific details that might prove useful. They would not know until the day of the competition which stance they would be required to take on a given topic. Perhaps the best part of the preparation process was that they learned as much as they could to convincingly defend or dispute their assigned stance. Of course, in real life we do not fill a file box with valuable information before jumping into a debate. These days, the validity of the information source might be questionable. (Think fake news, trolling, and propaganda.) Meaningful dialogue is an exchange of ideas, thoughts, opinions, or knowledge in which case accuracy matters as much as words.

Each of us owns the accuracy of the information we share. As challenging as it can be, it is necessary to sift through the information bombardment to find the truth and facts. Before you choose your words, choose your source of knowledge wisely. This reminds me of statistics classes where I learned how data can be skewed to make a point. A recent example would be how COVID deaths per 100,000 people is a more accurate measure of how individual nations of varying sizes are coping with the mortality of the virus than simply the number of deaths.

Debate, dialogue, and devil's advocate – how do you identify with these words? Do you use your words more for conversation, argument, provocation, or lecturing? At some point, each of these positions may serve your intention. Self-reflection may be useful to ensure your position reflects your values. You might also ask others their perspective of how you represent yourself in conversations. Do you adopt one of these styles over another routinely? If so, why? What purpose and who does this serve?

Polarity with Words

To reinforce the impact of your word choices, look at the choices as polarities – opposing poles. In doing so, we create sets of binary choices. You can either debate or lecture. Create a dialogue or play devil's advocate. Every time you enter a conversation, you make the choice of which role you will play. This overview is relevant to your inner and external voice. Your external voice represents how you converse with others. Alternatively, you might also reflect on how you hear these words and how much power they yield when you hear them. Fleshing words out in this manner helps to illustrate that there are always at least two choices and they may have quite different impacts.

I offer some common polarities that arise with word choices. Let us examine how each may be presented and received and how you might determine which option is the best in a particular situation. Consider which of the poles represents your go-to position in a conversation. Both your approach and your words are choices you will make.

Words of Praise and Words of Judgment

There is so much to consider about words of praise. Oftentimes, we do not truly register words of praise, although we vigilantly listen for words that condemn or judge. This is born out of a more natural inclination to look for what is wrong as opposed to what is right. Volumes have been written about the power of positive reinforcement. To bring harmony at home and in work settings, the suggested ratio is 5:1 – positive to negative feedback. However, most people who live in "fixer" mode at work or home remain on high alert for what they can amend, and inadvertently offer the negative over the positive.

Many adjectives may feel like praise but can represent judgment – or at the very least, can be representative of someone's values. This is heavily dependent on the context of the conversation. Adjectives attached to what one is working on (a project), or a person's stated goal, are more likely received without a sense of judgment. Adjectives tied to other things can lead to judgment. Here is an example when speaking with children: When a toddler puts his candy wrapper in the trash, you could say, "Good boy" and thereby only offer your judgment of him as a boy – good, in this instance. Or you could say, "great job putting your wrapper in the trash," in which case you are praising the action and his intention, without any implied judgment.

Words we use that may indicate judgment or negativity around an issue include "problem, struggle, and hard." When you state that something is a problem or a struggle, you imply that you have judged the circumstance and determined how it aligns with your values. In this case, you are suggesting that the circumstance that is a problem may conflict with your values. This may not be the case at all and warrants an exploration of values and consideration of what this "problem" means. For example, if I say, "Asking for a raise will be a problem," I am judging the effort. I may be assuming the effort conflicts with my value of not being confrontational. When I fully explore the situation, I may determine I value recognition for my work even more than the potential discomfort of a confrontation.

Words of Curiosity and Words of Indifference

Children are in a constant state of curiosity. This is one part of childhood that adults might want to recapture. We can use our powers of observation to spark our curiosity about a change in energy, tone, gesture, or volume. The best words for expressing this curiosity is to simply state, "I'm curious..." or "I'm wondering..." and then tie directly to what someone said, or what you observed. For example, "I am curious about how your energy changed when you mentioned your day at work. What's coming up for you?"

We use different words that might signify curiosity. You may say things such as, "I think..., I'm not sure if..., I wonder if..., I am uncertain..." Each of these phrases are prompts for deeper exploration. Conversely, you may offer words that are more apathetic such as, "I don't think..., I doubt if..., I don't really care if..., I'm not sure why..." Though these phrases represent a level of indifference, they are also verbal prompts to satisfy curiosity about what is valued. These statements speak to underlying beliefs and values that could be paramount for personal growth.

The best antidote to any potential expression of indifference is to remain in a place of curiosity and allow your questions and the words you choose to support your interest. I will share how this played out during the early days of the COVID-19 pandemic.

I was halfway around the world and away from my parents when everyone began sheltering in place. When I asked my father questions about changes they were making and how things were going, his responses were laced with indifference. This concerned me. My best approach was to remain supportive, non-judgmental, and extremely curious. I would say a lot of, "Tell me more about that…" and if we were talking about limits to his usual routine, "Tell me how that makes you feel." I believe my curiosity helped move him from being indifferent to being more curious himself about next steps and potential impact.

Words of Accountability and Words of Blame

The word that most accurately and succinctly speaks to accountability is "will." "I will" says that one is taking responsibility and owning an action. There are many supportive words of accountability to listen for and choose such as *outcome, learning, success, expect, expectations, reflect, path, actions, goal, progress,* and *commit.* These are all words that may provide insight into values and the terms by which one may measure oneself.

Other ways we express ownership is in how we say what we "have" to do and "get" to do. Speaking in terms of what one "gets" to do as opposed to what one "has" to do implies ownership over obligation. "Having" to do something implies a burden or obligation. So often what we refer to "having" to do is quite far from a burden. Additionally, this impacts those we converse with, especially if they feel a part of the perceived burden of what you "have" to do.

When the value is to be accountable, it is best to avoid words that shirk ownership and place blame. Words such as *should, must,* and *ought* all deflect the power to someone or something else. When one chooses these words, an exploration of the values that these words represent is beneficial. If you say, "I should make an effort to work with my colleague," You are suggesting a value of non-ownership, which is demonstrated by the words choosen. However, if you say, "I will make a greater effort to work with my colleague," you own that decision and can tie it back to a value of collaboration.

Words of Confidence and Words of Doubt

The words *will*, *can*, and *I am* are assertive, affirmative expressions that exude confidence. Choosing these words directly ties the topic to values. For example, "I will finish this paper on time," speaks directly to my value of timeliness. "I can check that action as complete by the end of the week," asserts with confidence the value of achievement. Saying, "I doubt I can get that done" or "I am not sure that will work" or "I tried" or "I don't think so" all represent doubt. When you use these expressions, you are potentially not aligned with your values. An opportunity exists to explore where these feelings of self-doubt are coming from and to assess how they relate to values and underlying beliefs.

To quote Yoda, "Do. Or do not. There is no try." *Try* and *if* are other common words used to bridge the gap between doubt and confidence. When you refer to *if* you are able to do a thing, as opposed to *when* you will accomplish a thing, you insert uncertainty. This presents an opportunity to understand if word choice come from a place of doubt, fear, or lack of ownership.

Words That Truncate and Words That Extend

Some words cause a pause or an end to a discussion. They create a transition to another topic or simply the end of the existing one. The most powerful of these words is *no*. A close second is *but*. The use of *but* can halt a conversation, especially if what follows strays from the intent. In recent years, there has been a surge in adopting *yes, and* responses. This has been used for improv and creative brainstorming and is taught as a leadership communication technique. The premise is that instead of shutting down the conversation with the *but*, you open it up with *and* as the joiner.

Forbes Coaching Council had one of the many Internet articles on this topic titled, *Leading With A 'Yes, And.'* It asserts, "'Yes, and' is a powerful leadership tool because it allows for affirmation and collaboration: two major traits in today's leaders." (Brown, 2017). In some circumstances it may be appropriate to respond "yes, and..." and leave it at that, making *and* a question that sparks further thought.

When someone frequently chooses *but*, they may have ownership issues that require addressing. *But* serves as a deflection and is oftentimes a joiner to an excuse.

For more on polarity, I recommend the father of polarity thinking, Barry Johnson. His book, *Polarity Management: Identifying and Managing Unsolvable Problems,* outlines the construct of polarity thinking. He provides tools for navigating paradoxes or dilemmas by identifying the upsides and downside of poles. This leads to creating concrete actions to maintain a balance within any given polarity. I find these frameworks extremely useful in my coaching practice. By the time you are reading this, he should have another book out that explores polarities in politics around the world. I was privileged to read a chapter on the 2016 elections in the U.S. which provided a valuable perspective (Johnson, 2014).

The Last Word Flag

Last Word

I find it difficult to know when my response does not need to be the final one. I have no trouble not having the last word when in a conversation where I need to further contemplate the discussion. Conversations where I would very much like my point understood and accepted are challenging. This is where one waits to raise the last word flag. Sometimes placing that flag can feel like closure to the conversation – at least for the person who stakes it.

The best way I have found to overcome this need or potential shortcoming, is to check in with the other person. "Is this a good place for us to end?" or "Have we covered this topic fully?" Perhaps it is even more important to hold space for the other person by pausing to allow for his reflection and actively listening. It is much easier to do this when I am conscious of holding the last word flag. With the flag in my hand, I can determine if it truly is my intent to have the final word, as well as what purpose that might serve. The visual of the last word flag helps me with the same contemplation in emailing and texting.

What You Say and What is Heard

Although this is really an overlay for the entire book, there are some common phrases and words that I would like to call out. You may intuit that some of these tie back to the defensiveness section (see page 33). These days it seems quite common for people to lead with how busy they are. This leaves me wondering about their intention. When most every conversation you have with an individual either begins with or is peppered with how much they have on their plate, there is much to consider. Some potential thoughts are:

- Is this a cry for help?
- Are they truly overwhelmed?
- Is this a way to show value?
- Are they defending their time and energy?
- Do they realize this is how they represent themselves?
- What value does this bring them?
- Will there ever be a conversation when they do not present their busyness?
- Is being busy one of their most important values?

Consider when you hear the word choices in the following statements:

- I have so much on my plate.
- I'm slammed.
- This is a crazy-busy time.
- I'm as busy as ever.
- I'm juggling so much lately.
- I'm running on all cylinders.
- I'm burning the candle at both ends.
- You wouldn't believe how much I've got going on.

What is the person really saying? You might interpret in this manner:

- She is truly busy.
- He appears busier than everyone else.
- She will always be busy.
- He is always overwhelmed.
- She has difficulty managing the demands of her life.
- It is important for him to share with others how busy he is.
- She values being busy.

Is this you? If you frequently hear yourself saying these types of things, ask yourself why. What is your intent? What purpose do these expressions of busyness serve? If you were seeking to set boundaries, consider words that more directly tie to that need. For example, "I have so much on my plate right now, I will not be able to fully participate." Or "I'm so completely overwhelmed, I'm afraid I may not be as present as I would like right now." Own your place in the productivity scheme of things. Own your plate. If you are seeking support, then say so. Words matter and clarity does, too.

Monosyllabic responses also fall into this category, particularly when used routinely. This is another use of words that causes one to wonder about the true intention of the responder. The most common example is, "Fine." On the TV show *Madam Secretary*, there is a scene where the protagonist's new chief of staff says "fine" when she tells him about this huge solution she had spent days developing. She starts deliriously laughing and asks, "Fine? FINE? That's all I get? Fine?" Right before she walks away, he replies, "I had a code language with the guy before you. 'Fine' meant 'Thank you for not messing up.' So, thank you for not messing up."

When you receive a "fine" response, you are wise to consider what the person is really saying. She may be saying:

- Whatever you are discussing is "good enough" for her.
- She is not really attached to the discussion or the outcome.
- She has no opinion and is generally in agreement.
- She has an opinion but is too busy, irritated, or disengaged to give it.

The problem with this one-word response is that much is left to interpretation. A more direct, clear, and carefully chosen response would be better for both parties. This way intent is understood and interpretation is not necessary.

REFLECTION

If you lean toward monosyllabic responses, regularly or occasionally, consider:

- Why do you do this? What more do you have to say that you are leaving unsaid? How do your brief responses align with your values? What is your intent when you answer in this manner?
- Examples: When I ask about something and your knee-jerk reaction is to say "fine," consider beginning your response with, "It was…" or "I am…"

If you hear monosyllabic responses frequently consider:

- How could you frame your questions differently? What sort of response might solicit additional feedback? Is the other person comfortable in the conversation? If not, how could you put her more at ease?
- Tell the other person that you are interested in understanding more fully and ask what more she can share with you.

> "Saying nothing sometimes says the most."
>
> EMILY DICKINSON

Silence

I invite you to choose silence more frequently.
Choose silence when your words will serve no purpose.
Choose silence when your presence is more impactful than your words.
Choose silence when you are truly listening.
Choose silence when you desire to offer space to another.
Choose silence when you have no words to serve the other.

STORY: HONORING SILENCE

Upon reviewing these thoughts on silence, a friend offered: *"This reminds me of the classes I teach at the Juvenile Detention Center in Montana. At a staff meeting before I had taught my first class, my boss talked about how silence can be a really useful tool in our classes and, knowing that silence isn't my strong suit, I really held on to that advice. After teaching many classes, I realize that it's so, so true. Especially when you're talking about something heavy, which we often are when we are sitting in a jail classroom. Giving a kid the space and time, through silence, to think and form their thoughts into words is a game changer."* —Olivia Round

Habitual Words

"The other day at work I was like 'this is going to be a long day.' And like when I first got there, I noticed like everybody else seemed to be like crazy busy." (Possibly uttered by my daughter at some point.)

Some habitual words are downright irritating. Habitual use of the word "like" can start to sound like fingernails on a chalkboard. Many young adults have no idea how often they use this word in conversation. Obsessive word use is similar to a tic. It happens unconsciously and persistently. Another example is "you know." I know that one of my overused words is "awesome" and I intend that this is the one and only time it appears in this book. I am aware and work on this. Which words hijack your vocabulary?

Phrases are another potential repetitive use pitfall. There are some that you enjoy hearing repeatedly. The risk is that they might lose value in overuse or eventually not be heard. There is some overlap to the "busyness" section here. Let us use "I'm sorry" as an example. When you hear this repeatedly from one individual, you are suspicious of their intent and might question their sincerity. Here are some reflection prompts:

- Is he obsessively sorry? If so, why is this?
- Is he only this way around you?
- Does he accept blame that is not his?
- What purpose does this serve?
- Is "apologizing" a value?
- Are you misunderstanding his intent?
- What is his true intent?

The only way to really know any of this is to ask. Ask where his apology is coming from, and what his intent is. Oftentimes, those who over-apologize are not truly accepting any blame. Their words have more to do with insecurities and beliefs that only they can fix. If you are this person, seek to understand why this is a go-to phrase for you. Pause to check intent before you offer your next, "I'm sorry." Are you really? Should you be? What do you truly wish to impart to the other person? Choose words that represent your intent.

Here are some considerations for reframing the habitual "Sorry."
Sorry I had to bother you – TO: Thank you for helping me.
Sorry for being late – TO: Thank you for waiting for me.
Sorry I didn't get that – TO: Thanks for getting that.

If you really do need to apologize, consider these guidelines:

- Do not require anything from the recipient.
- Do not use the word "but" at all.
- Do not include any blame on others or processes and systems.
- Do include what you will do to rectify.
- Do learn from the mistake.

Even heartfelt words require consideration. "I love you," are words we all hold dear and wish to hear. Of course, we want them to be said authentically and from the heart. Perhaps, there is no such thing as too much of this sentiment. However, you might periodically check in with those you love and offer deeper, more meaningful, and specific love messages. Here are some examples:

- I love that you just said that.
- I love that about you.
- I love you and our relationship.
- I love being with you.
- I love and appreciate you.

A MESSAGE FOR "TALKERS"

When I was younger, we ate dinner at exactly 6 p.m. every night. I have two sisters and a brother. We lived in a world with many rules — one of which was that we spoke only when spoken to. Each night at dinner, my father would go around the table asking each child to tell about his or her day. My brother was incredibly quiet and rarely had anything to say. When it was my turn, I felt as though I had so much to share about the day that I spoke very rapidly. I did not want to omit the tiniest detail. In my mind, I should have been able to cover my brother's unused time as well. Rarely did I end up expressing all that I wanted to share. To this day I believe that was the beginning of my speaking very quickly.

Here is what I have learned about being a "talker." Having a good story to tell comes in handy in social settings. You can leverage this skill to be more interested than interesting. This requires asking powerful, engaging questions of others. You have all met the introverted significant other of a friend who requires a lot of effort, the one you have to engage with questions before he feels comfortable opening up. Extroverts can be entertaining and must be diligent about choosing stories wisely and not repeating themselves. We can ask the same questions about our stories as we do for word choices.

- What purpose does the story serve?
- Is it aligned with my values?
- Have I used it before? Have I used it too frequently?
- Will those to whom I am speaking gain anything from this story? What might that be?

Slang

When and with whom is slang appropriate? Figuring this out is not as clear as it may have been decades ago. This exchange was reported in the *Daily Mail* and created quite a stir internationally (Seamark, 2006). George W. Bush: "Yo, Blair. How are you doing?"

George W. Bush: "'Yo, Blair, they've got to stop doing this s***'". Not to be out done by President Bush in using slang with foreign leaders, President Obama famously called Prime Minister David Cameron "Bro." Trevor Eischen reported in *Politico* that, "Relations between the United States and Britain are so strong that President Barack Obama 'sometimes calls' Prime Minister David Cameron 'Bro,' according to an interview with Cameron in the *Daily Mail*." (Eischen, 2015).

The current President, Donald Trump, not only uses slang but resorts to name-calling almost daily. Emanating from the top office in the U.S., and with no apology for doing so, he has standardized hate speech and foul language. Words matter and the frequent use of vulgar words and phrases by a top government official with this level of visibility and influence leads to unprecedented acceptance and adoption.

This impact may be much greater than the commonplace slang

words often spoken by young adults, particularly in conversation with peers. This is not an exhaustive list and is meant as a general overview of how slang represents word choices that should be relevant to your audience. My kids and their friends offered the following words, definitions, and examples. Upon further research into the origin of slang words, I discovered that throughout American history, slang has evolved mostly through Black and gay appropriation (Monahan, 2012). Teens and young adults have leveraged slang to self-identify with certain groups or individuals.

Word	Meaning	Example
Basic	Mainstream	That frat boy is so basic.
Boi	Friend/boy	Erik is my boi.
Dart	Cigarette	Brook went out for a dart.
Dibs	To claim something	I have dibs on the ice cream.
Down	I'm in – I'd like to do that	I'm down to get lunch later.
Dude	Interchangable with bro or bud and used for any gender (though this is controversial due to its inherently gendered origin)	Hey dude! I just missed your call!
Extra	A lot or over the top (usually in a bad way) – dramatic	He's so extra.
Fly	Hip or cool	Looking fly as hell with that new shirt!
Ghost	Not reply or respond to someone	Kevin ghosted her and she's sad.
Hangry	Hungry to the point of being angry	Mom gets hangry so she always has almonds with her.
Hammered	Drunk	Steve has had too many beers – he's hammered.
Hella	Definitely/super	I'm hella down to go climbing.

High-Key	Into something and I want everyone to know (big-time)	I'm high-key loving this book.
Homie	Friend, buddy	Olivia is a real homie.
Kicks	Shoes	Katie got some fresh new Nike kicks.
Lit	Under the influence of any substance, or cool/ happening	This party is lit! Jason just took three shots and now he's lit!
Low-Key	relaxed or secret	I might quit, but don't tell Stacy. I'm trying to keep it low-key.
Salty	Bitter about something	I ate the last piece of pizza and Molly's salty about it.
Shade	To throw shade – speak poorly about someone/ thing	Mark doesn't like Jacob; he's been throwing shade about him all day.
Shook	Stunned or startled	The ending of that film has me shook!
Sick, Dope, Gnar, Rad, Sweet, Hard,	All meaning great, fantastic, wonderful, awesome, epic	Did you see that sick backflip? It was so gnar! Steve is so dope.
Slap	Referencing something you like, particularly music	That song really slaps!
Slay	Doing well at something	Brit slays at work; she is so productive!
Sus	Something suspicious in a bad way	This month-old milk is sus.
Whack	Not cool, messed up	I can't believe you got robbed, that is whack!
Woke	Politically correct or progressive and inclusive in a diversity and world view sense	My gender studies professor is so woke.
Yo*	Hey/hello	Yo! What's up?

* Yo is still popular due more to hip hop influence than President Bush.

I thought using them in a sentence might help you understand their meaning and make you laugh. Disclaimer: They are unlikely to be strung all together in this manner during a conversation.

1. I thought his whip was hard until I saw his kicks; they're not basic and if he sells them, I have dibs on them! *I thought his car was cool, until I saw his shoes; they are not mainstream (common) and I have first priority if he sells them.*

2. I'm Hella down to go climbing, but not to meet Dela, it sounds sus that she's so extra. *I'm excited about going climbing, but not meeting Dela, it sounds suspicious that she is so over the top/dramatic.*

3. I'm high-key slaying this slang! *I am definitely doing a great job with this slang!*

4. My boi is really hangry, but at least he isn't hammered and hasn't had a dart all morning. *My buddy is a level of hungry that has resulted in him being angry. But at least he isn't drunk and hasn't had a cigarette all morning.*

5. He was pretty lit last night when he ghosted Maryann and threw shade on my homie. *He was pretty intoxicated last night when he started ignoring Mary Ann and spoke poorly of my friend.*

Abbreviations pop up in social media constantly, here are some popular abbreviations:

IRL – In real life

YOLO – You only live once

FOMO – Fear of missing out

DL – Down low (Meaning the skinny on something or to keep things quiet)

BAE – Before anyone else

DM – Direct message

RN – Right now

My B – My bad (I am at fault)

FB – Facebook

IG – Instagram

GOAT – Greatest of all time

BC – Because

Another category of slang that the brevity of social media may be impacting is abbreviated words such as sitch (situation), convo (conversation), obvi (obviously), and def (definitely). Some old words have new meaning. "Hooking up" does not refer to connecting your printer and "trolling" is not what single men do at nightclubs. The main recommendation is to know your audience. Slang is **not** appropriate in all conversations, certainly not with elders or in most work situations.

Speaking to Loss and Grief

My best friend, Pamela Herrmann, lost her second daughter, Lily, full term on Thanksgiving Day. This was one month before I was to deliver my daughter. I had no idea what to do or say. I was eight months pregnant and could not go to her because she was 1,200 miles away. I was incredibly hormonal and now petrified that I would have the same outcome. I had no words. I honestly cannot recall anything that I may have said in the days and weeks that followed. I still cannot imagine which words would have made any difference. As time passed, I recall Pam sharing how some words and actions had a greater impact than others. I have asked her to summarize some of the words and phrases that were not helpful, as well as those that may be best to hear in times of such pain.

📖 STORY: PAM'S RECOLLECTIONS

Any traumatic loss provides you with an odd measurement of the relationships around you. It took years to put order to my thoughts about my family and friends' response during this time. I finally understand it is an unrealistic expectation that because someone is close to us they will magically understand what to say and do. I was certain that everything they did in response was in direct proportion to how well they knew and loved me.

I realized almost immediately that nothing could be further from the truth. I didn't hear from some of my closest family in the days that followed and didn't learn until much later that they didn't know what to say or were afraid that if they said something it would only cause more pain. One of my sisters said, "The good news is, it is not like you knew your daughter." I think what hurt about that statement was that my emotions and experience felt minimized. I became very private about my feelings after that. My sister loves me and would never intentionally hurt me, this was just her way of saying that it could have been worse. Part of my journey was to seek to understand the spirit of those around me.

It has been over 20 years since this loss and I rarely think of how those closest to me failed to support me in the way I wanted, rather I hold very dear the acts of kindness from acquaintances. This was the true gift. Neighbors who I barely knew were stepping up and taking care of me and my family as we struggled to regroup. One in particular rose above everyone else in her generosity of time. KC would call me every day and ask how my day was going. Sometimes I just sobbed on the phone and she would just sit and listen. To this day it makes me cry to think of how desperate I was to have someone that I could unravel with, knowing that I could not share this primal level of pain with my family and close friends. It was too scary, even for me.

But what KC taught me is something I have been able to extend to other people around me who were experiencing grief. I would hand them my card and invite them to call me any time of day or night and I would do what KC did for me; I would be a lifeline on the other end of the phone.

Grief is a very lonely and isolating experience, even when you share the loss with someone else, you're truly all alone with your thoughts and fears. Supporting those around you during grief can be as simple as reaching out and letting them know you are there. Check in as often as you can and ask them,

- "How is your day going?"
- "I just called to check in because I was thinking about you."

- "You're not alone, I'm right here with you."
  This is the most generous gift you can give someone, the gift of your time.

Many years later Pam introduced me to Lisa Solis DeLong, one of my closest friends now. Lisa lost her son Justin when he was 15 and after a 10-year remission of leukemia. Shortly thereafter her fourth child, and second son, Jacob was diagnosed with the same cancer. She wrote an inspiring book about her experience called, *Blood Brothers: A Memoir of Faith and Loss While Raising Two Sons with Cancer.*

Her experience may have been the conduit to the bright light she exudes today. She suggests that, "Grieving people need inspirational mentors, new memories, and good listeners." She has also facilitated Death Cafés (an international movement) and has met many people in various stages of dealing with death and grief.

Lisa and I met to discuss how words matter in times of grief and she shared her thoughts, which I capture here. When you are in the presence of someone with fresh grief, it is important to consider several things. Do you already have a very good rapport? Are you able to sense whether they want to talk about their loved one? Are you sure that the words you choose will not be about you and focus solely on them? Are you coming from your heart and is your main intention how you might serve this person?

Lisa recommends these word choices:
1. Tell me more. This might play out in real life like this:
   - "How many children do you have?"
   - "Four kids; my oldest passed away last summer."
   - "Really, *tell me more…*"
2. I grieve with you as nearly as I can.
3. I am with you at heart (Lisa's go-to phrase in person and in notes).
4. This is a tender time.
5. I am holding you close to my heart. *(This is one of Lisa's favorites. She said this to an elderly friend recently whose 60-year-old*

son was diagnosed with leukemia. The friend replied, "I like it there.")

6.   Be gentle with yourself.

It is incredibly important to remember that such an interaction is not about you. If indeed you have no words, then remain silent. A hand squeeze can speak volumes. Do make sure to make eye contact. This way, you are still acknowledging that you are aware of the person's grief.

Here are a few things to avoid saying, as they serve no purpose for the recipient. Lisa's family heard these types of sentiments frequently:

1.   He's in a better place.
2.   God needed another angel.
3.   You are so strong; I could never handle this.
4.   You just need to have more faith.

When I asked Lisa about grieving during holidays or family events that brought memories rushing back, she shared this perspective: "We were at a dear friend's wedding a couple of months after Justin's passing. I felt like I was walking around with my arm cut off, in great pain, with blood dripping everywhere I went."

Some people key in to recurring or ever-present grief and offer kind, supportive words. Others appear unaware that this is a tender time. This is the perfect time to be fully present for another being and choose words that engage them on their terms. You might lead with, "I suspect this is a tender time, would you like to talk about your son? I've heard so much about him. I'd love to hear more."

Lisa conveyed this story as well:

"Sometimes there's a hidden gem in a conversation. I remember a couple of years after Justin's passing, I was at a gathering and intersected with a young woman who had known him in junior high. She approached me delicately and said, 'I just want you to know how dear Justin was to me. He was a great kid. I had a crush on him. He was my first kiss and I was his.' Here is the catch to an encounter like this: Timing is everything. If I was in fresh grief, known as mourning, this conversation could have flattened me. But in this moment, I was ready to receive her message. By this time, I was better equipped to handle this information and the emotions attached to it. I had learned that how I responded to my emotions was a choice. I had made this a kind of mental practice. I could focus on thoughts of love, *how wonderful, he experienced something many people never get, he enjoyed some healthy and youthful fun,* which led to feelings of joy and appreciation. Or, I could have focused on fear-based thoughts of lack, *he died too soon, he shouldn't have died so young, I was cheated, he should have had many more kisses,* which would lead to frustration, helplessness, depression, and anger. I didn't know how to do this at first, but Justin's death had cracked me open emotionally and spiritually. Because of him, I learned to pay attention to my thoughts. Thankfully, I had this understanding before the encounter with Justin's friend. I understood that it took a lot of courage for her to approach me. I hugged her and thanked her for telling me. It gave me a glimpse into his life from a perspective I would otherwise not have known. One of the greatest gifts a grieving person can receive is a positive or funny story about their loved one. This can also come in the form of a note or letter, which can be read in private so the grieving person can decide whether to read it right then or wait for a more emotionally stable day."

When in doubt, do two things: 1) Check your heart – it knows what to do and say and 2) Check in kindly with the other person, with a touch, or an acknowledging glance in a way to assess if words would be useful. Most importantly, be personally correct and do not make the encounter about you. The last thing a grieving person needs is to take care of your messy emotions.

Divorce or Split from a Long-term Relationship

When a couple splits-up or divorces there can be feelings of loss. This is another time to choose your words carefully. As is always recommended, assess your intent first and make sure the words you are considering are not about you.

I was married for a short time in my 20s. When I left my husband, the responses from friends and family confused me. Their words did not seem supportive and did not seem to be about me. What I came to realize was that my situation provided a mirror to others. I could tell by what they said that some people were assessing their respective relationships. This presented as questions to me about being sure ("Are you sure you want to leave? Are you sure this is best in the long run?"); and needing to know why ("Why do you think you have to do this now?"); and desiring more detail ("What exactly went wrong?"). I clearly recall feeling as though the person I was speaking with was reflecting on his or her circumstances.

As this is a type of loss, you should observe the same considerations for word choices. When you are fully present and coming from your heart, you will be able to interact with the other person in a manner that is supportive and not judgmental.

Sometimes words are not enough. In this case you might choose action over words. Consider providing gift cards. Gift cards for restaurants or movies are very helpful. You could even utilize reputable food delivery services so the person you are supporting can order in. While delivering meals can be helpful, sometimes too many or the wrong items can cause more work instead of ease to the recipient. Most importantly, do not ask, "What can I do?" The person hurting likely has no idea; and if they do, will not want to be a burden. It is best to call with a plan and limited choices. For example, you might call and say, "I would like to bring over baked potatoes, salad, and some chicken soup either Thursday or Friday. Which day is better for you?" This provides the opportunity for your friend to say, "We already have some chicken soup, or I do not care for potatoes." If you are unsure of what is best to make for a meal, ask someone closer to them for ideas.

Hate

When 9/11 happened, I was at Sundance Resort in Utah about to facilitate a weeklong workshop. The leadership team delayed the start of the workshop, and I remained there for the week. My sister was with me to care for my two children. We took them to a candlelight vigil in a town nearby. When we arrived, we heard a local dignitary admonishing what he had heard and observed locally in the previous 48 hours. Apparently, some of the local people had been saying "hateful" things such as how the people of New York City deserved this attack. The official very strongly said, "No one needs our hate!" My five-year-old son asked me what the man meant. I will never forget hearing those words or the emotion of trying to unravel it all in a coherent explanation to my son. The acts of terror on 9/11 were born out of hatred and there we were witnessing even more hatred by Americans. These words have popped into my head many times over the years as I have witnessed interactions in person and through the news. This is a clear example of the power of the words we choose.

Hate serves no purpose, plain and simple. My husband and I very consciously avoided using this word at all around our kids. We treated it as a swear word. We did not say or allow our children to say things such as, "I hate vanilla ice cream" or "I hate that game." These sentiments would have been a lead up to saying the same about someone who offended them at school. Kids are not born with any sense as strong as "hate" implies and I cannot imagine a reason why we should teach them to own this feeling. It is much more beneficial to teach them to consider various viewpoints and to express their dislikes in a reasonable, respectful manner.

When "hate" is an expression used at an early age, it will undoubtedly show up in adult life. Eventually, it will seem appropriate to "hate" a particular actor, TV show, situation at work, or even a person at work. It is one word that snowballs into feelings and expressions that serve no good intent.

PART TWO: INCLUSION, EXCLUSION AND JUDGEMENT

The world gets both larger and smaller as technology advances. We have access to more people around the world. We have the resources to learn more about other cultures daily. No more waiting for National Geographic to come in the mail. I frequently have days where my coaching clients call in from countries across the globe. We can see each other and share documents and pictures in the moment. This all makes the world seem so expansive and at the same time, smaller and smaller. It feels smaller because we can reach out and touch another soul so easily. We can connect with others from another country with different habits and rituals. When we open ourselves to our immense differences, we are back to feeling the expansiveness of the world. There are so many people unlike me. There is so much to learn from and about others. I am such a small part of this universe.

In America, hate crimes have been on the rise since 2015. The New York Times quotes Derrick Johnson, the president of N.A.A.C.P. "The level of tribalism that was being fueled by presidential candidates, the acceptance of intolerance that has been condoned by President Trump and many others across the country has simply emboldened individuals to be more open and notorious with their racial hatred." (Eligon, 2018). I believe we have learned that we have not come as far as some thought in honoring inclusion. That is one perspective. Others may suggest the progress was a delusion at best. This applies to women, people of color, those of different national origins, all gender identities, old people, indigenous people…the list is almost endless. There will not be an end for as long as our words and actions exclude others. I heard a colleague, who happened to be the Director of Inclusion for the nation's largest healthcare provider, say, "Diversity is being invited to the party, inclusion is being asked to dance." For the last few years, it has become apparent that inclusion is more lip service than anything else. This must change and each of us owns our role in this change: Every day, with every action, with every word. This is *not* where Grandma's Rule applies – "If you do not have anything nice to say, do not say anything at all." This calls for words and actions that align us with all souls in an equal manner. It requires us to speak up.

Being politically correct (PC) is not particularly a good thing in these politically divisive times. I propose that everyone focus more on being personally correct. The new PC. When we are personally correct, we are living true to ourselves and exemplifying our personal values. This sets us up for choosing personally correct words. As mentioned in the first chapter, your values must be your guiding light. When they are not, you risk not being PC, either the original definition or my new one. And, if your values are not founded in inclusion, acceptance, and love for all, your "personally correct" behavior may be offensive. This can also lead you toward "isms" – racism, sexism, ageism and so on.

Whether you hold an unintentional bias or are misaligned with your values, you forfeit any claim to correctness when you choose divisive words. At minimum, this requires two things: 1) You assess your values and beliefs, owning any inherent biases, 2) You educate yourself. This next section will tease out some basic education on words that affect isms, gender identity, and other cultures. An entire book could be dedicated to this important area and I apologize for only scratching the surface on each of these topics.

Racism

If I told you that certain words may be offensive to people from other nationalities and races, would you still use them? Do your words minimize another being? I have been in a conversation where someone called an Asian person "an oriental" and when corrected (kindly and with the intent to educate), the individual chose to stand by their ignorance. She maintained that everyone she knew said "oriental," as if that made it right. This type of denial happens with alarming frequency.

In *Witnessing Whiteness: I Need to Talk About Race and How to Do It*, Shelly Tochluk takes a close look at what needs to change, even before we can contemplate the right word choices. She states, "Unfortunately, many of us choose a color blind, transcendence-seeking optimism that ends up stifling the honestly difficult dialogue we need to have in order to deal with very real racial dynamics that continue to play out in our interactions." (Tochluck, 2010). Tochluck offers some extremely powerful questions for those of us born into white privilege to contemplate. She also talks about the racial scripts or recordings that play out in your head, regardless and because of your race or ethnicity. (Return to Chapter One for tips on changing the voice in your head.) Tochluck offers a deep dive into how to interpret and change these recordings in Chapter Seven of her book. *Witnessing Whiteness* wraps up with very concrete examples of how to witness whiteness and how to build a witnessing culture. I offer these resources to build a solid foundation for words that are inclusive. I have great hope for how actions and words will heal all that divides us, so that we are united for the good of all.

When I started writing this section, the news story of two Black men arrested in a Starbucks popped into my head. There are many daily examples of racism in this country. This incident happened on April 12, 2018. Rashon Nelson and Donte Robinson went to a Starbucks in Philadelphia for a business meeting. Within minutes of arriving and before their meeting associate arrived, they were asked to leave for not ordering. I have met many people in Starbucks and regardless of whether I ordered, I have never been asked to leave. No white person would be. Two bystanders got involved: Michelle Saahene was the first person to speak up and Melissa DePino filmed the interaction with the police and the subsequent arrest. The video went viral and has over 13 million views and counting. Previously strangers, Michele and Melissa went on to form an organization called *"From Privilege to Progress"* – P2P (www.fromprivilegedto-progress.org). Together they created a national movement to deseg-regate the public conversation about race. P2P calls on all Americans to walk the path to antiracism by learning, speaking up in their every-day lives, and amplifying the voices of people of color on social media. They have popularized the hashtag #showup as a call to action for all.

The following was shared on Michelle and Melissa's Instagram @ privtoprog. These words were a part of a graphic created by Danielle Coke, who goes by @ohhappydani on Instagram, Twitter, and LinkedIn. Visit her "activism through illustration" on her website: https://sohappy.social/. Danielle is a graphic artist whose work has really taken off as she highlights the inequalities toward people of color.

The graphic depicts six greeting cards with the following state-ments that outline microaggressions. Michelle and Melissa offer, "Most of the time these statements are made with good intentions/ intended as compliments – but that's what makes them microag-gressions: Comments that subtly (and often unconsciously) express a prejudiced attitude toward members of marginalized groups. In this case, we're talking about Black people." Danielle's insightful com-mentary provides concrete rewording suggestions.

1. "You're so pretty for a Black girl!" Normally said when a Black woman is actually beautiful even though she has darker skin! It implies that Black women are inherently unattractive. **Use instead:** "You are so pretty!" The End.

2. "You're so articulate!" Normally said when a Black person uses 'proper' grammar. This implies that Black people are inherently inarticulate. **Use instead:** Nothing – let's just not!

3. "No, where are you REALLY from?" Normally said when a person of color says that they're American (but doesn't appear to be at first glance). This implies an exotic nature. **Use instead:** "Tell me more about yourself!" That way they can choose whether to share.

4. "Your name is too hard to pronounce so I made you a nickname!" Normally said when a Black person has a name that goes against stereotypical norms. This implies that learning how to pronounce it is an inconvenience. **Use instead:** "Please, correct me if I am mispronouncing your name."

5. "Is that all your real hair?" Normally said when a Black person has a hairstyle of any kind. This implies that we are incapable of growing a lot of hair. **Use instead:** "I love your hair!"

Insights such as these made me desire a deeper understanding of how we got here.

My research led me through many books and one particularly striking article in the American Psychologist Journal. *Pride, Prejudice, and Ambivalence: Toward A Unified Theory of Race and Ethnicity* by Hazel Rose Marcus of Stanford University is well worth a read (Marcus, 2008). My head spun less on my third time through this important body of work. It is geared toward encouraging psychologists to adopt a different understanding of race and ethnicity. From my white race perspective, there was so much to learn from this article. For the purpose of better understanding how word choices matter, I offer these excerpts from the article but encourage you to read it so that we can collectively contribute to the dialogue on race in America. "Race and ethnicity are not, as some may worry, inherent or essential differences among people; instead, they are sets of ideas and practices with powerful life-altering consequences for individuals and societies, but they are not inevitable. Very significantly, the patterns of ideas and practices associated with race and ethnicity can powerfully *influence* or constitute our thoughts, feelings, and actions; this does not mean they *determine* our thoughts, feelings, and actions. As intentional meaning-making agents, we can actively reflect on, incorporate, resist, and/or selectively and inventively synthesize the ideas and practices of race and ethnicity." Markus does a phenomenal job of unpacking how race and ethnicity as social distinctions are constructs born out of Western philosophical and religious thought. Where does all of this lead us? It leads us to what we each own and to how we can each choose to be personally correct – by intentionally choosing words that are not a source of prejudice, discrimination, or inequality.

There is another consideration before assessing the words you choose in an interaction with someone who is different than you. As was illustrated in the section on polarities, you have a choice in your approach and position before you even choose any words. If you are white, you should be aware of what is referred to as white fragility. Robyn Diangelo wrote a book by the same title, *White Fragility: Why It's So Hard for White People to Talk About Racism* (Diangelo, 2018). She does a superb job in teasing out the inherent blind spots of a white person. I would like to highlight her perspective on being colorblind. "Because no one can actually be colorblind in a racist society, the claim that you're colorblind is not a truth, it is a false belief. ... Given that the goal of anti-racist work is to identify and challenge racism and the misinformation that supports it, all perspectives are not equally valid; some are rooted in racist ideology and need to be uncovered and challenged." She suggests white people engage in the following behaviors, which I believe will be beneficial to informing the words you choose. The behaviors are: Reflection, apology, listening, processing, seeking more understanding, grappling, engaging, and believing. Let us look at two stories that illustrate the need for these behaviors.

I met Deven Parlikar in 2014. He has remarkable self-awareness, empathy, and compassion. These traits come out in most every conversation. In discussing the nature of my book several months ago, he shared these two stories that speak to inherent biases and misperceptions. We also explored how ignorance might play a role in people saying such things.

STORY: FORCED TO HYPHENATE

When our oldest was 2 years old, we flew back to Detroit to see my in-laws. We sat across from an elderly couple. They began talking to us, leading with, "So where are you guys from?"

My first answer was, "We're from San Diego." After that my wife, Medha, took over.

Man: "I mean, where are you *from*."

Medha: "Oh, Rancho Bernardo." (suburb of San Diego)

Man: "I mean where are you originally from."

Medha: "Michigan."

Man: "Where are your parents from?"

Medha: "Oh, my parents are from Windsor, Ontario; that's where I was born."

Deven: "I think what you are trying to ask us is, 'What is your ancestry?' We are South Asian-Indian. Just out of curiosity, if we were white and we said we're from Michigan, would that have sufficed? I'm just curious why you probed with us."

Man: "I'm not racist."

Deven: "I know you're not. I often hear from others that I should be proud of being American and should not feel I have to hyphenate, but this is a classic example why I have to hyphenate our Americanism, by saying we are Indian-American. I don't see a lot of white Americans saying they are British-American or Italian-American; they are just American. But I have to be more specific and say I am Indian-American. Therein lies my frustration. Situations like this make me hyphenate."

Deven contemplated how this met the man's need, not his. Deven also shared a recent exchange with a close friend who said, "How could we do it differently with 'you guys'?" Deven pointed out the use of "you guys" in and of itself puts him in a box, indicating that he is different from a white person. We went on to discuss how word choices, such as those he shared, are born out of inherent biases and show up unconsciously from friends to strangers and everyone in between. Words matter and sometimes it takes thought and consideration to choose them wisely.

STORY: NOT SORRY

Deven was at the mall with his daughter, Meera, who had just started walking without her walker. She has an unsteady gait and a speech impediment. Meera was diagnosed with brain cancer at age 2. At the time of this story, Meera was about 5 years old. Deven and Meera were resting on a bench while his wife was in a store. A middle-aged woman approached and started a conversation. Meera was attempting to talk. The woman looked at Meera then Deven and said, "Oh my, what's wrong with her?" Deven recalls thinking her question came from a place of compassion and love, even maternal concern. Her tone and body language were very loving. He responded, "Nothing's 'wrong' with her. She had a brain tumor resected, suffered traumatic brain injury, so she is disabled." The woman followed up with, "Oh my god, I'm so sorry for asking you what was wrong with her. There is obviously nothing 'wrong' with her." She continued to apologize and even wanted to hug Meera.

Deven explained, "I know you did not intend your words to be hurtful. But for us and even her to hear that something is 'wrong' is very powerfully negative. Another way to ask would be, 'I see that she is struggling — what is she dealing with?'"

Deven is very articulate about the labor of love it has been for his family to learn from the twists and turns of their lives, as well as how others react. He told me that, "I had to experience it to feel it and only then could I change my own thought process and behavior." He thinks twice about his word choices when he encounters someone with what appears to be a disability. He suggests the following keywords and phrases:

- *If you don't mind me asking* or *if you are comfortable sharing with me...*
- *What is your child going through?*

- *I notice you are having some difficulty walking, what are you dealing with? Make your statement observation based.*
- DON'T SAY, "I'm sorry."

When someone offers, "I'm sorry" or even "I'm sorry you had to go through that" to Deven, he accepts this with a lot of grace. He may or may not counter with what he is thinking, "We aren't sorry. What we have seen through Meera's eyes has simplified the world for us. We have learned so much."

When we consider every conversation we have as a heart-to-heart discourse, we position ourselves to engage in meaningful conversations that are anti-racist. Each of us must commit to showing up fully aware of our inherent biases and how it may influence our words. Through this self-awareness we will be able to choose wisely and confidently connect with those who are different than we are. There are times when our silence is not beneficial and where silence is a stance itself. As a white person, I recognize these as times when I should stand up to racist relatives, co-workers, and friends and not wait for people of color to have to do it themselves. Together we can use our words to bridge the enormous gaps that separate us and prevent true inclusion.

Sexism and Ageism

I have been sensitive to sexism (discrimination based on gender) for as long as I can remember. I remain in denial that ageism (discrimination based on age) would apply to me anytime soon. My father has a lot to do with my view of both isms. He taught me at a very young age that I could do anything I put my mind to. At 18, I worked for his company, a firm that focused on electrical and mechanical engineering to build control houses among other things. I worked under the purchasing manager to procure supplies such as nuts, bolts, wiring, and steel. I was one of four women. One was the phenomenal secretary, Miss Grace, and the other two worked on the shop floor in the wiring department. In my role, everyone I interacted with was a man. Although I heard things daily that were sexist, my position was to give it no value. I have always perceived sexist remarks the same as racist remarks in that they are born out of ignorance. Sometimes they are also a reflection of insecurities and denial on behalf of the person speaking. This position has led me to stand firmly behind my own competence and not as a reflection of anyone else – man or woman. My father is 85 years old and still working. He is a valuable contributor at a company that was an offshoot of the company he sold. The owners and leadership team realize that his value defies his age. In fact, due to the sheer number of years he has worked in the industry, his relationships far exceed those of his younger counterparts.

Regardless of our ability to cope with them, words that are sexist or ageist are wrong. Many English words traditionally refer to men as hero, manager, mayor, congressman, policeman, chairman, and so on. Many idioms are male dominant such as best man for the job, man to man, one-man show, man hours, and many more. Occupational job titles that end in man are endless. They lead us to use the pronoun "he" in typical dialogue or when telling a story and referencing historically male-dominant occupations. For example, "I need to find a doctor so he can tell me what is causing the terrible pain in my arm." Additionally, there are common stereotypical job titles that infer a woman such as stewardess, salesgirl, and cleaning lady.

In my research, I stumbled across an article in the Gerontological Society of America journal called the *Gerontologist*. The research article, *The Language of Ageism: Why We Need to Use Words Carefully*, is the result of a study to understand how specific language communicates perceptions of aging. The study involves students who tweeted about their participation in the senior mentoring program. Ultimately, 12 percent (or 43) of the tweets had language perceived as age discrimination by the mentors. The bottom line was that, "ageist language is so ingrained in our day-to-day world that it's nearly invisible." (Gendron, 2016). The media and marketing of "anti-aging" implies aging is a negative experience and also drives ageism. I suspect with the baby boomers expanding the older cohort worldwide, there will be many more studies and resulting literature about this topic.

The same suggestion applies for sexism and ageism as with racism. I urge you to respond to what you witness. Although I may not have found it necessary to take on all the men who worked at my dad's company when I was 18, I am certainly clearer about the impact my words have. I own my ability to influence others. Sometimes this means educating them. It may mean pointing out their word choices and the effect they have on me. I do not believe any of us deserve the right to complain about injustices if we are not prepared to combat them. Step one is bearing witness and step two is speaking up.

Identity – Pronouns

Gender specific pronouns are as fluid as gender identity. Why is this important? Who does it impact? It impacts all of us. We are all part of an ever-evolving world and share in making it inclusive of all. By the time this is published there may be new suggestions on gender pronouns. I will cover the basics and invite you to continually educate yourself on this important issue. Again, why? Because it matters how we treat all beings. If someone does not identify with the gender norms I grew up with, does that make them or me wrong? Trick question. Neither of us is right nor wrong. We are different. Our humanity hinges on our acceptance of our differences.

Referring to someone by his or her name and pronoun is a form of respect appropriate for everyone. My research on the topic brought me to two great resources, *You're in the Wrong Bathroom!* by Laura Erickson-Schroth, MD and Laura A. Jacobs, LCSW-R and *Beyond Trans, Does Gender Matter?* by Heath Fogg Davis (Erickson-Schroth, 2017) and (Davis, 2017).

Erickson-Schroth and Jacobs outline some basic definitions, some of which I share here, and they provide some tips on word choices.

One of the main recommendations is that when you are in doubt, ask. A great tenet for all of us to live by and to better understand each other is to engage in dialogue with those who are different than us. These authors assert, "Trans people would generally prefer a respectful conversation about their correct name and pronoun than to have someone make a mistake based on an assumption based on ignorance."

Although some basic vocabulary follows, you may not recall this when you need to. So, the best way is to inquire, "What are your pronouns?" Or "What pronouns do you use?" as opposed to "What are your preferred pronouns?" Calling me *Mrs.* Short is not my "preferred" honorific, and she/her are not my "preferred" pronouns, they are the ones I use. They are the ones to which I identify.

Basic vocabulary on gender:

Term	Definition	Use and/or Example
Cisgendered	A person who does not identify as transgender	Born with a vagina, she identifies as a girl
Deadnaming	Calling someone by a birth name that no longer identifies them	News articles that refer to Caitlyn Jenner as Bruce Jenner.
Genderfluid	Fluctuating sense of self, identify as both male and female	My professor told students to use any pronouns they saw fit, including he/she/they, when addressing him/her/them.
Gender identity	Internal knowledge of being male or female	Outside of my genitalia, I identify as a woman.
Gender-neutral	Applicable to both male and female genders	The use of "they" to refer to an individual that does not identify as a man or a woman.

Gender nonconforming	A person (trans or cisgender) whose appearance and/or behavior challenges expectations (e.g., a feminine boy or masculine woman)	A person born with a penis who has long hair and prefers to wear skirts over pants.
Genderqueer	Identify as both male and female — a spectrum of masculinity and femininity	My friend who uses "she" pronouns but likes to acknowledge the male energy she gives off.
Intersex identity	People born with physiological and/or hormonal characteristics that do not match traditional binary sex classifications	
LGBTQIA+	Lesbian, Gay, Bisexual, Transgender, Queer or Questioning, Intersex, Asexual or Allies, plus countless other queer identities	
Misc (pronounced misk)	Gender-neutral	
Mre (pronounced mystery)	Gender-neutral	
Mx	Gender-neutral	
Nonbinary	No sex identity labels	
Queer	Not heterosexual (intentional vague)	
Sexual orientation	Who you are attracted to	
Transsexual	A person who emotionally and psychologically feels they belong to the opposite sex	
They/their	Gender-neutral	
Xi/xir	Gender-neutral	
Ze/zir	Gender-neutral	

(Erickson-Schroth, 2017 and Davis, 2017)

I had the pleasure of speaking with Davia Spain for a firsthand account of common misperceptions, respectful word choices, and those that hurt or are considered insensitive for transgender persons. Davia transitioned four years ago in San Francisco. She is currently a musician and performing artist in Los Angeles. She explained how difficult it has been to get her parents to use her pronouns and name. At one point, her parents told her, "You will never be that person to us, and you will always be who you were to us." She has had to stand her ground and explain that if her parents choose not to use her name and pronouns, then they will not truly know her. Through consistent conversations that she refers to as "hard and crunchy" with her family, she is working through the ongoing process of unlearning and rewiring. She spoke of the value of giving space for joyful reflections, which she has done with her parents in reviewing childhood memories. She shared that the language around who she is has changed a lot in the last 10 years. She views her family's ability to adapt as a test of compassion. She has relentlessly used the words that are important to her to plant the seeds for her parents' transition into fully knowing her truth. Sometimes that has involved using words that helped them feel as uncomfortable as she was feeling. It occurred to me that what Davia was describing was her effort at transparency to help with her family's transparenting, and how the dialogue must continue to evolve.

Davia explained that for the most part, she is passing as a woman and is therefore misgendered less. However, she does still have circumstances, one very recently, where people are quite aware of her pronouns and choose not to use them. It's exhausting. Constantly educating others and being on guard for hurt takes a lot of energy.

Davia suggests that everyone use "they" until they know someone's pronouns. She reinforces that the correct pronouns should be used whether the person is in your presence or not, while you are speaking of them. When asked of any particularly hurtful words or phrases Davia shared these: *Tranny, he/she, man in a dress.* Perhaps most impactfully, she told me that, "Language is how violence is enacted on us." Words matter.

Davia agrees with the recommendation that cisgender people offer their pronouns rather than wait for a trans person to initiate that themselves. For example, if you are a leader facilitating an orientation, have everyone introduce themselves with their pronouns, regardless of whether there is someone in the room who "looks" trans. Cisgendered people must do the work themselves. This is the same approach white people and men in the previous sections should take. Use your words well rather than put all the emotional labor on another person.

I had the opportunity to connect with a lifelong friend, Margie Gilmore, who has been with her partner for 16 years. They have a 15-year-old daughter and 12-year-old twins, a boy and a girl. They live in Southern California in what might be considered an accepting environment for the LGBTQIA+ community. As we were reviewing some of the content in this chapter, she shared a few thoughts on the importance of word choice. When her children were little they often heard, "It's impossible that you don't have a father, you can't make a baby without a dad." The two moms would assure their kids they did not have a dad, who would typically be a part of caring for them and instead, there was an anonymous donor who helped give them life. They often educate their community around the terminology that fits their family make-up. They find themselves explaining that a dad or father is someone who plays a role in your life and that it is possible not to have one of those. Sometimes word meanings need to be explored even before word choices.

While most of us grew up with the Golden Rule of "Treat others as you want to be treated," their children are growing up understanding the *new* Golden Rule, "Treat others as they want to be treated." This starts with asking questions and listening to others first. The simple change from "treat others how you would like to be treated" to "treat others how *they* want to be treated" is so much more inclusive.

Margie summed this up beautifully, "That simple word change creates a shift in humankind." It is so encouraging to learn of an environment where children are exposed to a rainbow of words that values and validates all.

Support for Those on an Alcoholism or Substance Abuse Journey

I have limited experience with individuals who struggle with addiction. My gut tells me that the best word choices are steeped in sensitivity. This is a very tricky topic, wrought with disclaimers. The journey of alcoholism, or substance abuse, is a very individual experience. There are levels of relationships, from acquaintances to family members, that dictate word choices. Family patterns with loved ones, spouses, children, and parents can complicate matters. Personal contemplation must preempt any conversation. What is your intent in the conversation? What is your approach? Why? Research suggests that anyone who has not been on this journey himself or herself will not fully understand what an alcoholic is going through (or has gone through).

An online search on the Alcoholics Anonymous (AA) site, as well as Al-Anon (support group for loved ones of alcoholics), did not yield any keywords for consideration in conversation. I turned to the incredibly bright son of dear friends, Sandro Cima, who is eager to help others along this journey. His insight will help you contemplate your words, keeping them true to your intent and ensure you deliver them compassionately.

I have expanded my knowledge through my research and in conversation with Sandro Cima. Sandro was a Recovery Counselor at a primary treatment center for alcoholism and addiction. He reports having learned so much in this role, from his personal journey and daily as a sponsor. First and foremost is that the impact of all conversations is relevant to a person's current status and it's incredibly difficult, if not impossible, to know where she is at any given moment.

This makes it particularly challenging for the driver of the conversation to navigate sensitively. As Sandro puts it, "No one has walked a single second in the other person's shoes." It seems this is a good place to start. Assume you know nothing. Know your own heart – this is the foundation of your approach.

Sandro shares that he once heard alcoholism explained as "The same instinct to run from a saber tooth tiger is what drives me to drink." The power of this instinct is hard to imagine if it is not experienced firsthand. The best any of us who are interested in connecting with someone who is experiencing alcoholism or substance abuse is to learn more through organizations such as AA or Al-Anon.

Sandro pointed me to specific sections in the Alcoholics Anonymous Book that offer some key words for consideration. Here are the highlights from Chapters 8, 9, and 10. Chapter 9 ends with three mottos: "First things first, live and let live, easy does it." This is good advice in any circumstance. One key point in Chapter 8 is the importance of fully understanding the illness of alcoholism. A lack of understanding will cause thoughts such as, "Why is this person so unthinking, so callous, so cruel?" It is suggested to make every effort not to condemn the alcoholic family member. Instead, accept that he is very sick. One suggestion is to, "Treat him when you can, as though he has pneumonia. When he angers you, remember that he is very ill." The intent of this chapter is to reinforce the futility in nagging an individual about what he must do. This harkens back to never fully understanding what the individual is going through. The recommendation is to make every effort to get your loved one to bring up the topic himself, and to remain non-critical. One example dialogue between a husband and a wife is provided as follows, "Tell him you have been worried, though perhaps needlessly. Show him you have confidence in his power to stop or moderate. Say you do not want to be a wet blanket; that you only want him to take care of his health. Do not crowd him." (Alcoholics Anonymous, 2001)

It seems appropriate to understand a few of the basic tenets offered by AA. One is "I'm not in control of people, places, and things." The Serenity Prayer, written by Dr. Reinhold Niebuhr, is widely accepted by AA is "God, grant me the serenity to accept the things I cannot change, courage to change the things I can, and wisdom to know the difference." Another tenet of AA is mutual respect. All interactions are based on this, in that everyone owns her experience and comes from a place of not owning or truly knowing the experience of another. These two principles are important to all of us in every situation in life. If we desire to converse heart to heart, we must start here.

Sandro speaks of how words frequently sound like what he calls "kidnapping." Although this can be literal, it is mostly through words that pressure one towards help. In this circumstance, the individual with the addiction is not driving toward the solution. The wrong approach can result in a buildup of resentment.

We reviewed some words or phrases that are not helpful and others that may be. A key takeaway is that one who has not walked in the other's shoes is unqualified to provide advice. The best support is a sponsor or an AA meeting where successful recovering alcoholics are prepared with nonjudgmental support.

As we discussed the nature of this journey, Sandro spoke of "receptive windows." These may be times when one is more open to conversation. He suggests that depending on the relationship and the frequency of conversations, there may be more of a willingness or ability to converse about the journey as time goes on. Again, every journey is very individual, and it serves no purpose to compare one to another.

The keywords he suggests are as follows:
1. "I support you."
2. "I will support you when you're ready."
3. "I trust you."
4. "I want the best for you."
5. "I support you and part of loving you is wanting to see you do

well. I am willing to help you in any way to find others who
were in a similar situation and made it out."

6. "I can't imagine what you're going through, but I'm here for
   you and I'm willing to help you in any way I can."

7. "I want to see you well and thriving."

8. "I want the best for you."

Proceed with caution:

1. "How long have you been sober?" When one is doing well, she
   may love talking about her journey. If not, she may have feelings of shame and may even be compelled to lie. If this happens and she opens up to you, only discuss it once. This can be
   very exhausting for the individual and your job is to provide
   space and listen.

Very *unhelpful* things to say:

1. "I know how you feel." The bottom line is you do not.

2. "Can't you just stop?" This reflects your lack of understanding
   of this journey.

3. "Can't you have just one?" This reflects your lack of understanding of this journey.

4. "Will you never get high or drink again?" This reflects your
   lack of understanding of this journey.

The very nature of AA is that everything is *anonymous* and you
should always respect this. If you feel compelled to connect someone
to someone else, you must proceed with great caution. You could seek
guidance from someone you know well and you know has been on
the AA journey, to assess her willingness to speak to someone you
suspect needs assistance. If she is willing to speak to your friend or
loved one, and gives you permission to mention her journey, then you
can privately offer the connection.

This information will fill basic knowledge gaps and provide some
key words from which to choose. I encourage you to dig deeper into

resources if someone you care about is on this journey. As with many topics we have covered, what you say is not about you. Your word choices should serve the recipient well. What *is* about you is educating yourself further, owning what is in your heart, and allowing your words to set your good intentions free in service of another human being.

Chapter Wrap

Wow. That was a lot to unpack and some of it may have changed before this is even published. "Correctness" is ever evolving and we should be, too. Each of us bears the responsibility of what we witness. We own our responses. We own our word choices. This chapter offered many examples of situations in which you might find yourself. I am hopeful you will choose the right words. Whether you are more prone to debate or to dialogue with another, educate yourself so that your words are supportive and kind. Seek to understand which words might be "trigger" words for someone else. Educate yourself on the values, perspective, and needs of those who are unlike you. Assume that you may know little about the journey of the other person.

Several sections of this chapter bring up interactions that might be considered bias-driven microaggressions. Silence when you witness another person being wronged or when you hear something inappropriate, is microaggression complicity. Microaggressions, such as the words shared by Danielle Coke earlier in the chapter, are everyday word choices that represent implicit bias. We need to train ourselves to listen for these subtle digs or repetitive put downs. We may hear them from others or catch them in our internal voice. Our collective sensitivity to microaggressions that hurt people of color, LGBTQIA+ individuals, or anyone who is marginalized will help us rid society of such verbal indignities.

Regardless of how hard we work on improving, we may still get it wrong from time to time. There are two important points here. First, if you are the person offended by word choices, own the challenge of finding a kind way to inform the speaker. Second, if you suspect you have not chosen your words wisely, apologize. At minimum, **ask**! You might offer, "I hope I have not offended you, that was not my intent. I am still learning about pronoun use (or racially charged words, or sensitivity to addiction) – please help me choose better words. I understand how much words matter."

Having the courage to gain insight will serve you well at work, too. Workplaces are oftentimes where we encounter more people who differ in nationality, looks, religious beliefs, and gender. As we develop the ability to keep judgment in check and respect others for who they are, our interactions in any environment will reflect our values. In Chapter Four, we will assess the challenges and word choices specific to the work environment.

"No matter what anybody tells you, words and ideas can change the world."
JOHN KEATING (ROBIN WILLIAMS IN DEAD POETS SOCIETY)

Chapter FOUR

WORDS THAT CONNECT US AT WORK

PART ONE: HEALTHCARE SETTINGS

I wrote 95 percent of this book before the COVID-19 pandemic started. It was edited in the spring of 2020. So much is changing in healthcare as I put on the finishing touches. Even where and how patients are seen is changing. Telemedicine has taken off and, in many cases, replaces in-person interactions. It seems appropriate to begin this chapter on the words we choose at work in clinical settings. Patients and family members who find themselves in a clinical setting are rarely without anxiety. The words used by everyone who interacts with them matter. Many healthcare organizations use communication frameworks that clarify expectations of staff. You will find an overview and resources for the common frameworks of AIDET, SBAR and TeamSTEPPS in the appendix.

The shortcoming of any framework is the absence of common sense. Frameworks are not necessarily scripted, or exact messages. They frame the interaction and provide some key guidelines to incorporate. For instance, the D in AIDET stands for duration because evidence indicates that people appreciate information about how long something will take.

You only need to watch the news to know that healthcare is an ever-changing, fast-paced, and complicated industry. This is where the use of keywords comes in. I find that certain words have a more positive impact on patients. Although I am not a fan of scripting, I support sharing these words widely for clinicians to choose from as appropriate. I will frame the interaction by way of the beginning, middle, and end from my perspective as a patient. Please consider whether these would be your expectations as a patient as well.

Patient Perspective

Beginning: When I am a patient, I like being acknowledged, along with any loved ones I have with me. I appreciate knowing the name and position of anyone who interacts with me. It is also helpful to know a few key things about them such as how long they have been in their roles, how many of these procedures they have performed, how long they have worked for this organization, and any bit of knowledge that will set me at ease.

Middle: This is the part where I want to know as much as possible about what someone is going to *do*, *why* they are going to do it, and *how* they are going to do it. Clear explanations and using terms that I can understand are essential to making me feel comfortable. I like to know how long things are going to take and what to expect, including timing.

End: I like to understand next steps and perhaps when we will interact again. I will likely express gratitude for information shared and time spent and I appreciate when others do the same. I find it appropriate for a clinician to express appreciation knowing that I have choices for where I receive my care. Sometimes I would like appreciation for the questions I have asked, my understanding, or simply my participation in my care.

Words to Choose and Related Actions

Beginning: The beginning of any interaction should include an acknowledgment of those involved and a proper introduction. While acknowledging patients and their loved ones, you could check for their preferred names and the relationships of patients and loved ones present. When introducing yourself, lead with your name, followed by your role and talk yourself and the team up. Here is how this might sound:

"Good morning Mr. Limp, who do we have here visiting? Do you prefer I call you Charlie, as I see noted on the board? Nice to meet you Mrs. Limp – I would like to tell you and Charlie a bit about myself. I am a respiratory therapist and I have been helping patients just like you for over 18 years. Helping you breathe better is my specialty and my passion."

Middle: Nothing eases anxiety more than knowing what to expect. A common misconception in healthcare is that things are unpredictable, so it is better not to give too much information or any clear expectation of timing. Many studies have debunked this myth. People want to know at least as much as you know about next steps and expect as close to the truth as possible. Regarding timing, I recommend you exceed your estimate so that you manage expectations better. For instance, if a test typically takes 90 minutes, tell the patient two hours. Your explanation is best if it is clear and does not include clinical jargon. Provide steps and pictures if appropriate. The only way to know if your explanation is understood is to **ask!**

End: Although I have interacted with clinicians who believe that gratitude is all from the patient, I adamantly disagree with this belief. I have witnessed many patients light up and relax a bit when they hear a clinician express gratitude. Patients have choices and healthcare is extremely expensive. It costs nothing and goes a long way to weave in a heartfelt statement of gratitude. My favorite is, *"Thank you*

for allowing me/us to care for you." Any version of this general sentiment will work and here are some other suggestions:

- *Thank you for trusting us to care for your mother/son/grandfather.*
- *Thank you for asking such great questions.*
- *Thank you for working so hard with me on your physical therapy –*
  you are doing great.
- *It has been my/our privilege to care for you.*

STORY: ANAPHYLACTIC SHOCK

A few years ago while on my way to a boxing class, my palms and
the roof of my mouth started to itch. I stopped at a gas station to purchase a
single dose of antihistamine. When I arrived at the boxing club, my face was
red and I discovered in the ladies' room that I had a full body rash. I decided
to seek medical attention. As I returned to my car, I called my husband to tell
him I would be going to the clinic. I chose the clinic, which was equidistant
to the emergency room, but was on the way to my home. As I pulled into the
clinic parking lot, I realized I had made a mistake. It was too late to try to drive
to the emergency room.

As I entered the clinic, the receptionist did not acknowledge me. As I stood
there, she looked down, around, and eventually in my direction. She offered
me a clipboard with forms and asked me to sit down and fill them out. As I
walked away it occurred to her that my needs might be more immediate. Two
individuals in lab coats then approached me and took me into the back area.
They asked me lots of questions and after initially putting me in a wheelchair
in an empty closet, they moved me to a room. My condition deteriorated rapidly. Several times I asked the two women working on me what their names
were. One of them inserted an IV in my left arm which caused blood to squirt
and drip. It seemed this was not something she did regularly. As my anxiety
increased, so did my curiosity about who these individuals were and what they
were doing. It was becoming more and more of a stretch to believe I was in
good hands. One of the times when I asked their names, a young lady who had
entered the room to provide something to them and was heading back out of
the room, heard my question. She hesitated at the door and said, "My name

is Emily." Hers was the only response I ever received. As I was beginning to lose consciousness, I heard the voice of my husband say, "Shouldn't she be at the hospital?" Miraculously, he had arrived and sat in the corner of the room. The next thing I knew, there were five men in the room who had arrived in an ambulance and firetruck. Two of the men told me who they were and what they were going to do, while asking me additional questions. I was going in and out of consciousness. They gave me an epinephrine shot and proceeded to load me into the ambulance.

Had the clinicians followed a basic framework for communicating with me, I would have been less anxious. When frameworks or communication routines exist, they are reliable in emergency situations. They should not be practiced periodically or only in slow times. Great communication in emergency situations might be even more important. To test my thoughts on communication, I turned to one of my favorite clinicians, Dr. Frank Reed.

A Family Physician's Perspective

I met Dr. Frank Reed while working at Community Medical Center in Missoula, Montana. At the time, he was the President of the Community Physician Group, a multi-specialty practice comprising of approximately 60 clinicians. He was also intimately involved in helping the group create its collective organizational values, something we worked on together. I knew from the moment I met him that he was a clinician who brought his full heart to every interaction. I have spoken about many of the topics in this book with him at one time or another over the last 10 years.

We have always agreed that self and social awareness, and empathy – key components of elevated Emotional Intelligence - are essential to any leader, especially those in healthcare. This includes all health professionals. During his 50-year career, Dr. Reed has endeavored to hone his emotional, as well as his clinical, skills. He is someone who can speak very deeply about what is required to remain authentic and to be true to oneself. I suspect this is reflective of his commitment as a lifelong learner.

We sat down to review the specifics of patient encounters and how word choices matter. What he shared with me was all experiential from his perspective as a clinician. Our conversation revolved around the personal work one must do to show up fully present and caring in a work setting. I have learned over the last 10 years that this personal work has meant everything to Dr. Reed. I know so few people who put such an emphasis on the self-knowledge needed to be consistently in the service of others.

There are several physician writers who speak to the nuances within healthcare and the patient-physician relationship. The works by Dr. Atul Gawande explore the challenges of healthcare worldwide using metaphors, analogies, and personal experience as a surgeon. *In Shock*, by Dr. Rana Awdish, navigates her remarkable near-death personal health issues and provides insight into the role compassion and intentional communication play in patient care (Awdish, 2017). Dr. Thomas H. Lee describes how suffering affects clinician-patient interactions. In *An Epidemic of Empathy in Healthcare: How to Deliver Compassionate, Connected Patient Care that Creates a Competitive Advantage*, Lee provides evidence for the importance of empathy in interactions (Lee, 2016).

I am honored to share a summary of Dr. Reed's reflections, based on our recent conversation. He reminded me that there are many challenges in healthcare, most of which start with the clinical environment. Clinicians face competing demands and many distractions; inadequate time being one of the greatest challenges. The healthcare environment is one that is often noisy and chaotic yet aspires to personal intimacy. This requires the clinician to be quite discerning to meet the patient where she is during each interface. Context might be the most important component of the interaction. Being able to fully understand the context of each interaction requires skills such

as appreciating the specific circumstances of the patient's life, pausing, listening deeply, minimizing the power differential, and remain-
ing present and authentic. I asked him about each of these and specifically what he did or said with his patients as a reflection of these
skills. I took the liberty to break them into the key components of
Dr. Reed's interactions.

Context Considerations: These are almost endless and relevant to
each encounter. Some examples are: How much ownership does the
patient have in his care? How much assistance is the patient likely to
have or need? What else is currently going on in his life?

Pause: Dr. Reed recommends a 30 second pause before entering
the examination room and interacting with a patient. These 30 seconds serve the purpose of gathering one's thoughts, taking a few
deep breaths, quieting the voice in your head, separating from the
last patient, and preparing to engage the context of the pending
interaction.

Opener: Dr. Reed leads with a salutation and then introduces himself if he is unfamiliar with the patient. For those he is familiar with,
he leads with some relational knowledge such as, "How are the kids?"
He then routinely asks, "How can I help?"

Listen: After that question, he listens intently until the patient is
through speaking. Dr. Reed's attention is on creating an environment
and appropriate relational space where the patient feels he is the only
person who exists at that moment. This requires non-verbal and verbal skills and attunement, including body positioning, adequate eye
contact, and appropriate proximity – not standing over the patient.
Part of listening is gaining knowledge of the patient's language level.
It also involves watching for shifts in energy and reading expressions.
Close observations often provide insight into what is not said.

Share: While there is usually specific clinical information to be ascertained and shared, this is also a time for the patient to share. This is the time for motivational interviewing techniques: Determining what is important to the patient to facilitate true shared decision making. It is also when the power differential might come into play. Older patients are more likely to acquiesce their power to the physician. The best way to minimize any perceived levels of power is to work towards putting people at ease. Dr. Reed does this with relational responses and connecting to the patient on a personal level. He also strives to avoid clinical jargon. Clinicians have approximately 10,000 words specific to their education, most of which are foreign to the average patient. The only way to truly know what the patient understands is to ask. He offered some keywords and dynamic questions to get to the heart of the patient's understanding. Here are some examples:

- "I am getting the feeling that my explanation may not be effective. Can you help me understand what matters most to you?"
- "We've just gone through several important things; I'd really like to hear from you what you heard."
- "What is most important to you?" (Asked *before* offering options for care)
- "How do you feel about what I just told you?"

Closing: During the discussion of next steps, Dr. Reed asks open-ended questions to assess for a deeper understanding. When he is unsure that a patient fully grasps next steps, he suggests more immediate follow up. For example, he might say, "What do you think about the idea that we get back together next week?"

One of the more remarkably misunderstood tenets of the patient-clinician relationship is that the patient assumes the clinical competence of the physician. Physicians do not have to spend time proving their competence to the patient. Their time is best spent proving they care for the patient, as this is *not* something the patient assumes and often perceives as the opposite in the busy office milieu. If a clinician does spend time asserting her competence, in the words she chooses and the general posture of the interaction, she is operating from a place of ego. This does not serve the patient.

When I was digging for any sort of framework or specific words, I particularly liked the metaphor Dr. Reed shared with me. "Like a chef, you do not use a recipe; you feel into the ingredients. I need to create a healing experience. That requires that I set the intention that they can feel me feeling them. I need to do this without overwhelming myself and I believe this is all part of professional empathy. All of these interactions must occur with appropriate boundaries."

I have always appreciated Dr. Reed's optimism and hopefulness. This is likely born out of his belief that relationship building, as well as self and social awareness, are learnable skills. He speaks eloquently about the healing transmission that occurs in the clinician-patient relationship. Most importantly, he fully understands that this begins with the clinician being aware of her own humanness and being able to center herself. The centering requires an alignment of the physical, cognitive, and emotional self.

Much can be lost in translation or misunderstood due to context. Here are some examples of what is said and how it may be heard. What would you add to this, either from the perspective of patient or clinician?

What is said	What is heard or assumed
The tests were negative.	This is bad.
The test results were positive.	Everything is OK.

📖 STORY: THE WORDS OF LISA'S PHYSICIAN

When the door opened, Justin snuggled closer to me as Dr. V entered the room. He was a small, thin man with a thick Indian accent and an unusual sense of humor, the kind that sometimes got him in trouble with the parents of fresh newborns, whose perfect birth plan did not include a saucy little Indian telling them their baby had a big nose.

"Just like his father," he'd say with a chuckle.

I knew him as kindhearted and often misunderstood. I chose him when Justin was born for his reputation as a thorough physician. I'd seen him care for the babies in the women's unit (where I worked as a nurse), with the zeal of a father and I respected him for that.

He walked in the exam room, put the chart on the counter by the sink, and started with, "Hello. What is happening, my friend?" Then he turned, took one look at Justin, and spewed, "Oh no, no, no. You nurses, you know how to take care of everyone else but your own kids!"

My eyes filled with tears. Justin was sick; very, very sick.

How could I, his mother, who sees him every day, a medically trained professional, not see how ill he was? I wanted to bang my head against the wall and scream. I don't cry easily, but the tears began to stream down my face.

Doctor V, realizing the lack of sensitivity in his choice of words, softened. "I'm sorry. Kindly let me examine you, Justin," he said.

I slid off the table, helped Justin lie down, and held his hand. His deep brown eyes studied Dr. V's face as the doctor, mumbling and shaking his head, palpated under his jaw, his neck, and then deep into his abdomen. Dr. V was pensive and brisk with his instructions.

"Take Justin to have blood drawn now, please. I will be waiting for you when you are done."

He gathered up Justin's chart and apologized again as I wiped my eyes and left the exam room trembling with fear and humiliation.

Justin was diagnosed with Acute Lymphoblastic Leukemia, the most common kind of childhood cancer. As the dust settled after this stormy diagnosis, I pondered the experience. I wondered why this brilliant physician who had devoted his life to saving children like mine was not in his brilliance when I needed him to be. His words were like a dagger to my wounded heart at a time when I needed cotton balls. It would take years of reflection and inner work to heal that wound.

It broke my heart the first time I read this story in Lisa's book, *Blood Brothers*. This was the day that would forever change her life. Although one might argue that the physician did not enter the room knowing that, he should have assumed that she was an anxious mother, desperate to know what was wrong with her son. If he considered her being a nurse as part of the context for their interaction, he should have positioned this in a positive way. He could have led with, "Does this little boy know how lucky he is to have a mom who is also a phenomenal nurse? Let's take a closer look at what might be bothering him." Accusations have no place when a clinician speaks to a patient. They serve no purpose and their only outcome is to make the patient or loved one feel even more poorly. While Dr. V did apologize once he observed Lisa's reaction, and he did offer to be waiting upon her return, these two actions alone were not enough to constitute effective communication. His words did not match his intention.

As Dr. Reed suggests, clinicians must develop a keen sense of self and social awareness. The impact of the words they choose can be devastating. In the busyness of the healthcare environment, pausing for even a nanosecond to become centered and present is the basis for finding the appropriate words.

I asked Lisa after so many years of reflecting on this scene how she would have replayed it from the physician's perspective. Here are her thoughts:

I think it is important for patients to be reminded that physicians are people, too. While I felt damaged by the encounter with Dr. V, I also saw him as a human being and was able to forgive him. If I had to replay that moment in time, I would like to have heard, "You are a good mother," or "I know you did the best you could," or "We will hold your hand through this process," anything that conveyed that my team saw me as the young mother of two small children in a crisis. What is difficult from the other side of the curtain is when our personal emotions get ahead of us in interactions with our patients. Perhaps, if Dr. V made a practice of checking himself in times of upset and had a practical, mindful tool in place for encounters like mine, he could have avoided the harsh nature of our interaction. He may have simply excused himself, stepping out of the room, regrouping, taking a deep breath and re-entering the space. I know this sounds unrealistic in a rushed medical setting, but I do believe that practicing self-awareness and effective communication skills are worth our time and attention.

Words matter.

PART TWO: ALL INDUSTRIES

Being of Service

The healthcare setting is certainly one steeped in relationships and service. The COVID-19 pandemic is teaching us more about being of service each day. The world has become clear about services that are "essential" and how each of us can be of service to others. Hopefully, we have all encountered the employee or leader who revels in being of service. Conversely, the odds are good that we have all encountered an employee who has no business being in a service industry. If being of service is an organizational value, as well as a standard of behavior expected, then several things must happen:

1. Leaders must model being of service to their teams, including the use of keywords.
2. Communications must tie to values, using keywords.
3. Everyone must be accountable to the same service standard and candid conversations must occur when observing a shortcoming to the standard.

Ritz Carlton and other high-end service industry organizations take the position that all employees will follow the same script. The Ritz Carlton's service motto is "Ladies and gentlemen serving ladies and gentlemen." When I worked at Four Seasons Hotels, there were some basic words recommended for use in conversation with customers. For example, when a customer asked for something a response should include, "My pleasure," or "I'd be happy to." These types of responses confirm the value of being of service.

About 20 years ago, the phrase "no problem" became popular and worked its way into responses from service providers nationwide. "No problem" implies that there may have been a problem, which the customer typically does not expect. And if there is a problem with a request, ordinarily the customer is not aware of it. When we request a service, we are mostly interested in what can be done and how it will be accomplished.

Example: I call down to the front desk to ask for additional pillows. The staff member responds, "No problem, I'll send someone right up." The person who knocks on the door with the pillows presents them and when I say, "Thank you," they respond, "No problem." I am left feeling that there may have been a problem and perhaps my request narrowly escaped being burdensome.

Let's use the same example as above but with different responses. I call the front desk to ask for pillows and the person on the other line says, "Absolutely, I would be happy to send them up." The person who delivers them responds to my thank you by saying, "It was my pleasure," or simply, "My pleasure." This interaction leaves me feeling that it was okay for me to make this request. I did not interrupt or burden anyone.

The adage I stand by is, "The guest or customer is not an interruption to our work, but the reason for it." Living by this requires displaying the appropriate actions and choosing the right words. Let us look at some choices everyone in business has.

Clarity

Some words are simply too vague and others are too descriptive. Some words leave the recipient with a lack of clarity. Words such as "some," "soon," and "a bit" do not communicate much while phrases such as, "It's a disaster!" exaggerate a situation beyond what is necessary. In these instances, check yourself for clarity. Are you being purposefully vague? Are you being purposely dramatic? If so, why?

Words such as "everything" and "everybody" beg further explanation or detail. We often use these terms to collectively represent a thought or belief. This can be problematic and exaggerated. When you ask a customer for feedback and they tell you that "Everybody was great" or "Everything was great," you need more detail. A follow-up question might be "What particularly made our service easy for you?" or "Who in particular, was helpful?"

When an employee tells a leader that everybody or everything was _____ (upset/terrible/bad – you fill in the blank), further exploration is needed. Have you ever heard something such as, "Everyone thinks this is a stupid idea. It is never going to work." What is the truth of the *who* and *what* of their story? And how does this person know? What is his or her truth? Does the speaker own the word choices or is he or she parroting others? This is a concept that Quint Studer looks at closely in his book, *The Busy Leader Handbook* (Studer, 2020). I would like to explore the word choices related to this.

ACTIVITY

Consider whether you are apt to use vague, general words or exaggerated ones. Think back to the last two stories you told. Answer these questions:

1. Can you identify any opportunities to use words that invoke clarity for the recipient?

2. Do you recognize a pattern of word choices that you should break and replace?

3. Can you recall a time when you spoke on behalf of an entire group – invoking "they believe," or "everyone thinks?" How would you rephrase this to represent only the thoughts you own?

> "To change a culture, the leaders have to change the messages people receive about what they must do."
>
> FRED KOFMAN

Great Leaders and Great Employees

Dr. Thomas F. Frist Sr., the founder of Hospital Corporation of America (HCA Healthcare) said, "Good people beget good people." When I worked at HCA, I enjoyed any opportunity to interact with Dr. Karl VanDevender, who was Dr. Frist's personal physician and is quite the HCA historian. Through the use of story, he brought to life the actions Dr. Frist Sr. took to provide healthcare founded on the principle that "Good people beget good people." This adage applies to all businesses and is important to employees, leaders, and all those a business serves. Living this relies on a foundation of shared values.

I had the privilege of working for another organization that led with the company values. This started during the interview process. After completing online tests geared towards Intelligence Quotient (IQ) and Emotional Intelligence (EI) an applicant may proceed to a series of five interviews. Each person along this route impressed upon the interviewee the values of the organization and asked very direct questions about the interviewee's potential contribution. They also shared their own stories of how they made a difference in the lives of others. This served the purpose of showing their values in action. I was honored to secure an invitation to the last interview, which was with an outsourced psychologist. As arduous as the process seemed, it served the organization and me quite well. In the end, we were both clear about my fit with this organization.

The day after finalizing the hiring details and formally accepting the job, I received a beautiful bouquet of flowers at my home with a note from the organization's founder welcoming me. I was anxious to be one of the great employees serving at this organization. The word choices of each interviewer and the welcome note intentionally set the expectation that everyone lives the values of this great workplace.

I have often repeated the saying, "The fish stinks from the head," to illustrate the impact of alignment that begins with the leader(s) at the top of any organization. The likelihood of "begetting" good people is greatly diminished if the top leadership is misaligned or does not always live the company values. This cannot be overstated. It begins with the words that leaders choose and the consistency with which they choose them well, not just on camera or at large gatherings – always. Let's break this down.

Leaders spend an enormous amount of time and money trying to get people to do things – to do them better, differently, ahead of others, more efficiently, and so on. Leaders get stuck using the same words and processes to influence others to change. Spoiler alert: People do not change and leaders bear a great deal of the responsibility for this. Behaviors change. There is a direct tie between the effort to influence change and the impact to the limbic system. Simon Sinek explains this expertly in his successful TED Talk, *Great Leaders Inspire Action*. With close to 48 million views, his presentation is the third most popular TED talk of all time. So, why aren't more leaders enjoying less effort to sustain change in their organizations or building better business models?

Why? Because "the fish stinks from the head." Many leaders and hardworking employees show up daily with good intentions, ready to do the right thing. When they fail to do as expected, to adopt new processes, embrace a new ideas, make requested changes in actions and on and on, there is one reason - leadership. Either the leader has insufficiently clarified expectations, not held everyone equally accountable, not fully owned the change himself (i.e. blamed others), or most importantly, failed to lead with "why." Leading with *why* inspires learning and triggers any combination of emotion, feeling or memory. The leader has not been intentional with his words to provide the needed clarity. He has failed to trigger the key functions of the limbic system. There has been no impact to one's emotions or memory if behavior is unchanged. Mr. Sinek's evidence suggests we lead with *why*, follow with a *how* that is guided by values, and anticipate the *what* that results from our actions. I have spent most of my career emphasizing *why* one should do this or that, leaning heavily on the related evidence of a practice, as well as the impact to the individual and those she serves. My values and principles have always guided me. This has not always been enough to effect change. *Why*, you might wonder. Here's a story:

When I was a novice leader, I recall believing that my leadership role meant it was my responsibility to explain what needed to be done and how it was to be accomplished. Of course, as I matured as a leader, I came to understand how erroneous and ineffective this approach was. Later in my career as a consultant and coach, I became aware of the pervasiveness of this approach. This is apparent on several levels. I have witnessed countless frontline leaders tell their employees only the *what* and *how* behind the work they were expected to do. Additionally, if the senior leaders have not properly expressed why they have solicited the services of a consultant or coach, then the team is left assuming that they have to do what I advise and how I advise it, regardless of the *why* I impart.

Oftentimes, as diligent as I am at expressing the *why* behind an expectation I propose the leader implement or consider, he only wants to hear *what* and *how*. The *what* and *how* are typically all that is shared with his team. I see this repeatedly as the go-to position of leaders. I suspect part of the reason is that they want to be bottom-lined on which evidence-based tactics will improve performance. Although this is a large part of what I am hired to coach on, the inability to grasp the *why* (which is really understanding the evidence) almost certainly determines the sustainability of what I impart. On the other hand, when a leader understands the *why* behind a certain process or tactic, he embraces it 100 percent. He is then able to articulate why he is asking the team to do something differently and engage them in the specifics of *how* and *what*. These kinds of leaders inspire their teams. As Simon Sinek illustrates, they engaged the limbic region of their employees' brains, thereby influencing their feelings and decision making.

Here is an example: For years, I have coached nurse leaders on how to do effective nurse leader rounding. Just as physicians complete "rounds" on their patients, or visit with them daily while they are in the hospital, nurse leaders also do rounds on patients to ensure the quality and safety of their care. I always lead with an explanation of why rounds are important to leaders. This includes saving them time, connecting them to their patients, and helping them keep their finger on the pulse of the care their team provides. Nurse leaders routinely report these three things as important to them as leaders, but I suspect not all of them hold these as priorities. From my perspective, the *why* represents what is potentially in it for them. Evidence supports that when nurse leaders effectively round their patients, their patients' perceptions of their care improves. Additionally, this rounding provides them daily insight into the strengths and opportunities that exist on their unit. Consequently, they have opportunities to coach their teams to provide the level of care that their patients expect. The rounding and coaching combination prevents service recovery opportunities that typically consumes much of their time. Their high performers look forward to the feedback gained from their patients. I have witnessed the morale of an entire unit improve when a nurse leader fully embraces this tactic. Indeed, the leader is operating proactively as opposed to reactively. But alas, not all nurse leaders embrace weaving daily rounding on patients into their routine.

Why not? My first thought is where did I fail to connect the dots? How did my discussion on the topic fail to appeal to their beliefs of how this change would benefit them, make them feel differently, and connect them to their purpose? What better words should I have chosen? How should I have varied my approach to meet their needs? Given the opportunity, I revisit all these possibilities and remain quite proud of my usual impact. But it is not always a 100 percent success rate. The organizations with greater success have stronger leaders at the helm. Ones who can reach the limbic systems of their leaders on a regular basis. Ones who are able to show their vulnerability with the words they chose. They chose words to be more inclusive, clearer about expectations, and specific about what accountability looks like for their organization. How can you do that?

5 STEPS to NOT Being Stinky

1. Know a person's why – his purpose (or your team's). Ask questions such as:
   a. What do you value about the current state of _____?
   b. How has this _____ (current state) impacted you?
   c. What is most important to you when we adjust expectations (or make a change to improve results)?
2. Then lead with the *why* behind a change that connects with theirs – be very specific about this. Use keywords such as:
   a. Doing _____ supports our value of inclusivity (or being of service, or providing value, or being efficient).
   b. From my perspective, doing _____ will give you back some time (or streamline your workflow, or allow you to focus more on _____ (a priority for her).
3. Dialog until you impact one or more of the following: Feelings, emotions, memory or learning. Use keywords such as:
   a. I shared my perspective, tell me yours based on what you heard.
   b. Tell me how you feel about this change.
   c. How is this different or similar to the last time we made improvements to change _____?
   d. What effect do you perceive this will have on the team?
4. Engage the person or team in establishing *how* (next steps). Use questions such as:
   a. What do you perceive the next steps to be?

    b. How do you feel you can work this change into your routine?

    c. What needs to happen first for us to be successful with this?

    d. Who else might this impact and how might we include them?

    e. What is your greatest concern about what happens next?

5. Engage the person or team in developing the ***what*** (the results they will own, the outcomes desired or expected). Use questions such as:

    a. I have shared our intended impact related to this change, what other results do you expect?

    b. What outcomes will be most important to you? Why?

    c. How do you suggest we track progress?

    d. What are your thoughts on the ownership of success? Who will do what by when?

I challenge you to assess your approach. Is it limbic-centric? Exactly which words make it limbic-centric? Do you need to revisit an expectation? Take it from the top. Always follow the five steps above at the beginning of something new. This is the first phase of leading with why. Next will be to adjust as needed, then recognize and address gaps in execution. You may be inclined to think this will take too long, but not following these steps is sure to lead to a vicious cycle of misalignment and unsustained change.

Successful leaders employ various ways to keep the organization's *why* at the forefront and revolving around values. This is always appropriate, not just during times of change. Charlene Li wrote *The Disruption Mindset,* which outlines the need for organizations to embrace disruption as an integral part of their business models. I spoke to her specifically about how to promote a values-based culture and she shared this story.

STORY: CHARLENE LI ON VALUES

When I was running Altimeter, we used to start staff meetings by inviting people to share how our company values played a role in their lives in the previous week. Sharing these stories gave us a glimpse into each other's world by illustrating how we lived our values. Storytime can be built into ceremonies of recognition, departures, staff meetings, and weekly communications. The key is to build it into the rhythm of your organization so people regularly gather and share stories that are meaningful to them.

We would start by inviting everyone to take three deep breaths and ask if anyone wished to share an experience where our values came into play. I recall one example of a leader speaking about how they were able to lean into being empowered. They wanted to do something very different but did not think that they had permission. They developed their plan and ran it by another colleague who reinforced that empowerment was one of our values and encouraged them to proceed. Another example that comes to mind revolves around our value of integrity. We had provided leadership training on how to have difficult conversations. One leader knew that the right thing to do was to have a hard conversation with a colleague and to do so in a way that the relationship would thrive. The person telling the story spoke of how their sense of integrity meant leaving nothing unsaid and proceeding with the skills taught in the training. They shared with the other person how anxious they were, as well as how angry they had become. They reported a conversation that was very candid and had keywords such as "Can I give you some feedback?" and "I'm not in a good place given our value of integrity and feel compelled to work through this with you." I especially liked when the leaders wove the values tightly into their conversations. The sharing of the stories served to keep our values present and to show each other how we were able to weave them into our day-to-day conversations and activities. Company values and the related behaviors provide a great foundation for choosing the right words.

Influence and Inspire Others

When I think of influence and what is written about it, Dale Carnegie immediately comes to mind. *How to Win Friends and Influence People*, his seminal work, has been around for 80 years and sold over 20 million copies (Carnegie, 2011). As a great orator, Carnegie valued words and their impact. I would like to use his nine basic premises to inform how the words you choose may impact your ability to influence others.

ACTIVITY

The nine premises are in the first column, the second column lists suggested words to use, and a third column is for you to contemplate how you would rate your current abilities in each of these areas. Rating your competence will inform where you may need to practice a different approach with impactful word choices.

9 Premises	Potential Keywords to Use	Rate Competence 1-10
Give people a fine reputation to live up to	You communicate very effectively, you are an expert at building relationships, you are easy to talk to…	
Encourage others to talk about themselves	Tell me about… Your children, where you grew up, one of your favorite jobs and why, how you learned to do _____ so well.	
Genuinely show interest in others	That fascinates me, tell me more. I did not realize that, please go on… I am interested in learning more…	
Don't resist people, agree with them first	I hadn't thought of it that way, please tell me more. I can see that, can we explore further?	

Appeal to the noble interests of others	I know _____ is quite important to you; I would like to learn more about ____.	
Talk in terms of the other person's interest	What is the best part about _____? When did you first become interested in _____?	
Make the other person feel important	It sounds as though you are the best at _____; your practice/attention has really paid off. That is amazing; you should be so proud. I am astonished.	
Ask questions instead of giving orders	Ask questions that start with "what" or "how" or "tell me about…"	
Use encouragement and make the other's faults seem easy to correct	I can see how that might happen… Seems that could have happened to anyone… This really isn't a problem at all or is the least of our concerns…	

Dale Carnegie's work is all about building relationships, which requires getting people to like and trust you. I believe this begins with liking and trusting yourself. Once this is the case, you can genuinely like others.

More recently the authors of *Crucial Conversations* published *Influencer - The New Science of Leading Change,* an important business book for leaders at all levels (Grenny, et al, 2013). While this book is really a manifesto on leading change, one of the main components is how to influence others, which applies to all of us. Grenny et al provide a framework that leverages both motivation and ability as it relates to personal, social, and structural constructs. Their six sources of influence are:

1. Help them love what they hate
2. Help them do what they can't
3. Provide encouragement
4. Provide assistance
5. Change their economy
6. Change their space

Each of these six sources of influence requires carefully chosen words and questions to have the greatest impact. Either of these frameworks can be very beneficial to your ability to influence others. Each component requires your word considerations for full impact, as illustrated in the chart on Carnegie's work.

Leaders' Words – "I Think"

I have coached a lot of executives over the years. At first, it was a pet peeve of mine to hear a leader say, "I think...." What always goes through my mind is: You are paid the big bucks to "know." I learned to appreciate that there are times the leader means that she "thinks, but is unsure" of something. Occasionally, a leader may choose "I think" to indicate to the team that theirs is only one opinion on the topic. When a leader routinely uses "I think," especially when providing information, this can be perceived as uncertainty.

Examples:
I think our sales are going to be fine in Q4.
I think our customers will appreciate this.
I think our team is going to hit it out of the park.
Omitting the first two words of each of these sentences would make the message stronger and represent more confidence. This goes beyond a pet peeve to something I passionately care about when coaching leaders. Sometimes we simply need to omit words from our lexicon.

Words that Undermine the Organization

There are commonly used words and phrases that only serve the purpose of denigrating an idea, person, or organization. Which of the following have you heard in your workplace?

1. You don't understand.
2. That will never work here.
3. We've tried that before.
4. You won't get support for that – they will never go for that.
5. There's nothing we can do about it.

These types of statements can be so discouraging especially when you are the new person at work. Even if you have been in your organization for quite some time, you should perceive these as morale busters. Such statements only serve to denigrate the value of the individual, a process, leadership, or the organization. If these are the types of words you choose, I highly recommend you consider your intent. These types of statements appear to have the intention to diminish others, promote the status quo (or even mediocrity), shun ownership, and stand on shaky values footing. I challenge you to do the following:

A. Stop saying any of the statements listed above.
B. Consider why you were saying them in the first place.
C. Call out others who say these things. Ask them why they say this. Ask them what they really mean. Seek to understand where they are coming from and commit to working toward better clarity and more unifying messages in the future.

Managing Up

Prior to my career in healthcare, I thought of "managing up" as how I shared information with my bosses. It represented how I kept them in the loop and leveraged them appropriately in order to do my job well. I believe this is still a pervasive definition of managing up. In healthcare, I learned a deeper meaning that is useful in most any setting. I would like to elaborate on this broader meaning and how it informs word choices. Here are two examples:

In late 2019, AT&T ran two different commercials that suggested "good enough" was not really good enough when choosing a phone company. One of the commercials showed a mechanic who spoke poorly of his track record and qualifications, leading the customer to wonder if her brakes were truly fixed. The other profiled a surgeon who told a patient he was "pretty good" at the pending procedure. Both presented the opposite of "managing up." Managing up in the workplace is the sharing of positive information about another person, place, or process. Every employer wants her teams to manage up the service they provide and manage up for each other. This is as simple as saying great things about the services and the team.

One of my tenets for managing up is a rule I mentioned previously. Grandma's Rule is "If you don't have anything nice to say, don't say anything at all." To offer anything that is not constructive serves no purpose. Conversely, managing up another person, place, or process serves the purpose of instilling confidence and reducing anxiety.

Some of the best examples of the value of managing up exist in healthcare. Who doesn't want to hear positive things about the team that is taking care of them, or the facility they are visiting, or the procedure they will be receiving? Telling me that you are an expert phlebotomist before you draw my blood absolutely lessens my anxiety. Hearing that my physician is the best in her field and that she has performed hundreds of the same procedures, serves the purpose of putting me at ease. Often, we hesitate to manage ourselves up fearing that it sounds like bragging. A distinction between the two is this: Bragging serves the person who is doing the bragging and managing up serves those receiving the information.

As you might expect, managing down creates the opposite effect. Hearing negative things about someone or something related to a service I am seeking causes me concern and potential angst. Sometimes the manage down is inadvertent and born of an intention to commiserate. An example would be when the nurse manages down the physician stating that "He is typically late in meeting with his patients, because he takes on too many in one day." Hearing this only serves the purpose of making me feel badly for being one of those patients requiring the physician's time. It makes me part of the problem. I would certainly prefer to hear, "Dr. Jordan is running a bit behind. He spends quality time with each patient and will be with you in less than five minutes. He is amazing and you are in great hands." These words help me appreciate the physician, understand his tardiness, and increase my willingness to wait without concern.

Managing up can still be how I interact with my bosses and keep them fully abreast of what I have on my plate. It can also include a positive outward expression related to yourself, your colleague, your team, or your organization. These types of exchanges are very powerful and promote healthy, supportive dialogue that is beneficial to all.

REFLECTION

A. Who can you routinely manage up to others?

B. What exactly can you say that is positive about your coworkers, your team in general, your organization, another team, your boss, a process?

C. What will you say to someone who manages down another person, process, team or organization? At the very least, you should seek to understand the intent of the speaker. Oftentimes, people are unaware that their words serve the purpose of denigrating and have a negative impact on listeners.

Recognition

Early on in my leadership career with Four Seasons Hotels, I was the recipient of feedback from a survey given to my staff. While the feedback to me as a leader was positive overall, my area of opportunity was providing more reward and recognition. At the time, I was in my mid 20s and held the position that receiving a paycheck was reward enough for me and should be for others as well. I worked long days and had much on my plate. Reward and recognition were not on the top of my list. The general manager of the hotel and one of my lifelong mentors, Stan Bromley, is a world-class thank you note writer. He asked me about my frequency for writing notes and my response was that I wrote many notes in a day, but all of them were to our guests. He challenged me to write a minimum of two thank you notes per week to someone who worked at the hotel. These could be any employees, not just those who worked under me. He was illustrating that everyone's contribution mattered and reflected in the high level of service we provided. After the first couple of weeks, I found that I easily got to the end of the week and had forgotten to write any notes. I began putting two notecards in my inbox at the start of each week. This was a physical box, which may be a foreign concept to some younger readers. There was a complementary outbox that I placed memos and mail for distribution. I would never end my week without writing the notes and moving them to the outbox. One could simulate the same routine by creating draft emails each week and filling in the recipient and the specifics of the recognition.

> TIP: I have also used a calendar prompt to draw my attention to weekly recognition. Create a meeting invite for yourself to stop and recognize others.

With the amount of people I supervised, this acknowledgment system still wasn't enough. Another leader suggested a visual, or a prompt, to ensure I showed gratitude to individuals throughout the day. I chose to hold three quarters in my left pocket at the start of each day. As I would thank a staff member or provide recognition for their contribution, I would move one quarter to my right pocket.

This worked so well as a daily reminder that I eventually changed to five dimes. Others were unaware of this easy prompt and I recall doing this for about a month before my daily expressions of gratitude became habitual. I have told this story many times over the years to other leaders during speaking engagements or one-on-one coaching. I have received consistent feedback that a visual prompt helps develop a meaningful habit.

Chip and Dan Heath cover recognition, along with many other great opportunities in *The Power of Moments* (Heath, 2017). They emphasize that recognition needs to be personal, not programmatic. This is a pitfall for many organizations. It takes a bit of creativity, and asking some direct questions about preferences, to devise a meaningful way to recognize others. Through various stories, they explore the positive psychology of providing recognition and how it also affects the giver.

Recognition can be as tricky as criticism. Recognition preferences vary greatly. Leaders should make it a priority to understand how their team members prefer recognition. Parents and spouses might benefit from this approach as well. Generational differences may also come into play.

One of the leading experts on Generation Y, Jason Ryan Dorsey, has studied Gen-Y preferences. He provides valuable insight in *Y-Size Your Business* (Dorsey, 2010). He has an entire chapter dedicated to the first day of employment and suggests that Gen-Y employees decide on their first day if they will stay in a job. He supports my premise that the only way to really know what will appeal to someone, specifically a Gen-Y'er, is to ask.

The best practice that I have witnessed is to make this a part of employee orientation. This could be as simple as a card the new hires fill out and forward to their team lead. Regardless of the employee's preference, the leader must always be authentic. The words you choose will support your authenticity.

The card could have prompts such as:

1. Do you prefer private or public recognition?
2. What are your top two criteria for recognition?
3. When appropriate, how would you order your preference of the following?
   - A handwritten note
   - An email
   - Extra time off
   - Candy or another food treat: _____
   - Recognition in front of my team
   - A trophy
   - Other:_____

What can make recognition tricky is a true consideration of the individual's mindset. Sometimes people with low self-esteem have difficulty hearing praise. When they hear compliments, they have difficulty accepting and relating the kudos to their actions. The giver of the recognition is not responsible for this, but an understanding of this position is helpful. The previously mentioned (Chapter One) ratio of 5:1 – positive to negative reinforcement – is a good place to start. You increase the chances of your positive message being heard by a factor of five if you leverage this ratio. There are several studies that support this ratio; chief among them is a study by Marcial Losada and Emily Heaphy, published in *American Behavioral Scientist* (Losada, 2004). Their work highlights business unit performance relevant to leadership feedback. Performance improvement reflected a 5:1, positive to negative, delivery of feedback.

Let us explore the impact of the words to choose when giving recognition. Assume that in each scenario my intention is to recognize this employee for her work on the project and to acknowledge that she had to put in extra hours.

Option 1.
Example: ***Thank you*** for staying late last night to finish the project.

Impact: My boss values people staying late and the timeliness of our projects.

Option 2.

Example: Thank you for *your contribution* to finishing the project last night. I *am sorry* that doing so ran into the evening. I *appreciate your commitment* to the *team* and to the *completion of this project*.

Impact: My boss values my contribution, my time, and my commitment to my team.

ACTIVITY

Think of someone who you would like to recognize for something she or he has done. Here are some prompts for your consideration:

- Should this be written or spoken? Choose written if memorializing this feedback might be important to the receiver. There will be more on handwritten notes in Chapter Five.
- If spoken, will it be in private or in public?
- What are the key things you wish to recognize? (Your intention)
- What are the keywords you should use to have the impact you intend?
- How do you wish the receiver to feel because of this recognition? How does this influence the words you will use?

STORY: THANK YOU FOR THE THANK YOU

I have mentioned Quint Studer previously in this book. Over his many years in healthcare, he has accumulated some remarkable stories. In recent years, perhaps due to his concern for physician burnout, he has focused on physician related stories. So often physicians are overlooked when it comes to reward and recognition.

He shared with me several anecdotes. One included a physician who personally went to the store to purchase the exact milkshake his 10-year-old patient desired. Another was about a surgeon who called her patients the night before their surgery to assure them that she was well rested and looking

forward to seeing them in the morning. She answered any last-minute questions and I am sure helped instill confidence and lessen anxiety. I wonder how
often these physicians are thanked.

Then he told me about the thank you for the thank you. When Quint was
the president at Baptist Hospital in Florida, which was a level one trauma center, there was a serious accident that involved many people. As Quint made
the rounds, he witnessed a radiologist who was leaving his shift through the
ER waiting room. This radiologist saw how chaotic the ER waiting room was,
particularly for the loved ones who were waiting for news. He stopped and
decided to be a runner to provide information from the ER clinicians to the
family members who were waiting. He did this without being asked and for
quite some time. Apparently, he did not see this as a heroic act. He was recognized in front of his peers the following month, received a thank you note
from Quint, and recognition in an awards ceremony. He proceeded to write a
note back to Quint thanking him for the recognition, sharing how much it had
impacted him. He told Quint that day was one of his best days as a physician.
I suspect the heart-felt gratitude he received illuminated the day. What difference can you make by recognizing someone's contribution?

Asking for What You Want or Need

Recognition is usually a passive experience for the recipient. It does
not necessarily need to be this way. It is appropriate to let others
know how you like to be recognized and to be specific and clear
about what you want.

After much research in my late 20s, I decided I desperately
wanted a new Subaru. I lived in the San Francisco Bay area at the
time. Without the benefit of the Internet, I was able to source the
best place to find the car I desired. I went to a dealership in Marin,
north of San Francisco. This was one of many times in my life when
an older male spoke to me in a condescending manner. After choosing my perfect car, we proceeded to his desk for what I thought was a
negotiation. Armed with all my preparation, and in a very confident

manner, I proceeded to state what I would pay. He condescendingly told me about their process, which involved four squares and apparently a man behind the curtain. After much back-and-forth and car dealer babble, I stood up and walked away. We had done all the paperwork, except for agreeing to the purchase price and terms. I did not allow my emotions to be involved in this negotiation. No matter how desperately I wanted this car, I also wanted to negotiate well. It was a learning experience and all car purchases since then have gone extremely well.

Not everyone enjoys negotiating. This is another one of those forms of communication that goes better when tied to values. Negotiating connects to one's self-esteem and self-awareness. Self-awareness equips us with a solid understanding of our strengths. Start by determining which of your values is important to a negotiation conversation, as well as which of your strengths benefit your position in the negotiation. For example, if I am negotiating for a promotion, I first assess why this is important to me. This assessment would cause me to look closely at my values. My assessment might reinforce that I have been excelling at my value of being of service and I may believe that I could have a greater impact with this promotion. Additionally, my value of collaboration may have served me well in my current position and I may have clarity around how I can leverage collaboration in the new position. Contemplation on my values and strengths will help me create the *why* and *what* of the negotiation conversation. The *how* will be determined by the words I choose. Will my words support a position that is defensive, supportive, insecure, believable, confident, unsure, demanding, or inclusive?

Effective word choice should thoroughly cover why, what, and how. Here are some prompts to help you frame a negotiation conversation:

1. Why is this important to me?
2. How will I articulate what is important to me and my value?
3. How does this align with my values?

4. How do my strengths support this negotiation? (In how I discuss the topic, as well as in support of what I'm requesting.)
5. What will the benefit be? To me? To the other person or organization?
6. What will be non-negotiable?
7. What are the key components of my position on this topic?
8. How can I leverage my skills and strengths?
9. What will my response be when the other person either agrees or disagrees with me?

I have been successful in negotiating by framing such conversations as win-wins. After clearly identifying my wants and needs relevant to my values, I create my position. I frame my position around my strengths and contribution. I tie this position to the benefit it will provide to the other person or organization. I use clear and direct language to articulate my position. I provide ample opportunity for questions and I am prepared to respond in a non-emotional, non-threatening, and concise manner. My preparation enhances my confidence.

STORY: ASK FOR WHAT YOU WANT AT ANY AGE

This is a story about managing up **and** asking for what you want. Several months ago, my daughter started a new job in a new city. She was only in the job for a couple of weeks before she realized that the organization would benefit from her contributing more. She had great ideas to improve sales, as well as processes. She created an outline of all the things that she had observed and her potential solutions. Then she asked for a meeting with her direct supervisor to discuss her ideas. Her supervisor was quite open to such a discussion and immediately proposed a meeting time. However, three different meetings were set and never kept. Meanwhile, another employee was given some of the duties my daughter had been speaking of and hoping to be assigned. She was quite frustrated.

A couple weeks later, she found herself on a two-hour drive with the manager who was her supervisor's boss. She did not wish to throw her supervisor under the bus in any way. As the conversation evolved and the manager asked her questions, she shared some of her ideas. The manager was extremely appreciative of her insight and energy for improving the business. She eventually did have to share that she had tried to communicate her thoughts to the supervisor. In the end, the situation was handled well by all parties. The result of the conversation with the manager was a meeting a few days later with the manager and the owner. The outcome of that meeting was that she had a new role and a raise.

There are several lessons here. The first is that she did not hesitate to manage herself up. She used her vision, her skills, and her solutions to impress upon her boss the additional value she could provide. She is 22 years old and one of only two women working at this organization. Another lesson is that she went into the conversation with her manager with great confidence and intention. One of her intentions was to not jeopardize her relationship with her supervisor. She chose her words very carefully. She did this again when she discussed the situation with her supervisor a few days later. The last lesson is that she was prepared and incredibly clear about what she wanted her contribution to be.

On a Team

Most of us have heard the adage there is no "I" in team. When working on a team, it is beneficial to consider your relationship to the other team members, as well as your relationship to the work being done. Speaking in terms of your own contribution and therefore your ownership is a great foundation. There are many things that can denigrate the productivity of a team. What contributes most to the success of the team is communication. The words we choose in communicating with our team may reflect our own values and consideration of the values of the team. In a perfect world, these two sets of values do not conflict.

When speaking on behalf of the team, it is best to use the pronoun "we." A continual use of "I" may create the perception that your contribution or work on the team is more important than that of others. The use of "I" should indicate when you are representing how *you feel,* particularly if there is conflict, or if you require clarity. The use of "I" relates precisely to what you own. When you are making a comment that's relevant to the team, use "we."

Be mindful of using the word "they" when referring to a team. Invoking "they" can lead to an us/them or we/they culture or a culture with a clear separation of ownership. This leads to blaming. This creates the perception that "they" or someone outside of the team is responsible for a decision or an outcome. There will not be shared ownership unless all relevant participants truly understand the *why* behind the decision. Decisions at all levels should tie back to organizational values. The organizational values are the *why*. For example, if an organizational value is excellent service and it has been determined that there are not enough cashiers during a routine busy time each day, you decide to adjust employee schedules. If you explain the decision in terms of meeting the value of excellent service, employees would be able to articulate to others why this change occurred. In the absence of this information, an employee may simply believe and say "they" changed our schedules.

I learned the concept of owners versus renters from one of my mentors, Quint Studer. In his most recent book, *The Busy Leaders Handbook*, he outlines this concept in Chapter 24, "Create a Culture of Ownership Inside Your Company" (Studer, 2020). A lack of ownership is modeled through "they" statements as indicated above. Quint offers some key leadership behaviors that lay the foundation for employees adopting an ownership position in their organizations. The main points are to model ownership, share financials, regularly solicit employee feedback, involve employees in the hiring process of their coworkers, allow those closest to an issue to find the solution, and continually connect employees back to the impact of their work.

Each of these suggestions sets a leader up for choosing the right words to complement and reinforce their actions.

📖 STORY: PULLING ON THE SAME ROPE

In 2005, as General Manager, I opened the largest luxury guest ranch in the state of Montana, The Resort at Paws Up. As is common with the opening of a new business, there were extreme challenges. Daily, I would hear employees say completely inaccurate things. I learned very quickly that in the absence of real information people revert to MSU. And no, I don't mean Montana State University. When information is lacking, people quickly choose to "Make Shit Up." If I was going to pull off all that needed to get done, I needed every person pulling on the same rope. This intention required a daily commitment to clear communication. Occasionally, I would ask "Where did you hear that?" or "Who said that?" The team would often tell me that I had said it, which was rarely true. These are a few lessons that I learned to inspire ownership among the team:

1. Keep the leadership team and all employees abreast of the details as you know them.
2. Create opportunities for frequent Q&A sessions.
3. Recognize employees for their contributions. Create an atmosphere of "We are all in this together."
4. Ask direct questions of employees about their needs.
5. Routinely ask leaders and employees to provide their understanding of a detail and then fill in any gaps.

"Alleged" Difficult Conversations – Not Just at Work

There are too many frameworks for having difficult conversations to name. Let us start with an explanation of what a difficult conversation may be. What determines that a conversation will be difficult? Is it because we suspect there are opposing opinions? Is it because you will share information that was previously unknown? Is there a potential for hurt? Is there a potential for disagreement? Will there likely be strong emotions? Is the topic something that makes you uncomfortable? The answers to these questions will help you determine if the conversation may truly be difficult and why this might be the case. Who will make the conversation difficult and what can you do to mitigate the difficulty? How can you prepare more and plan to choose your words wisely?

This gets us back to intent. If the perception is that a conversation will be difficult, step one is to contemplate *why* this will be the case. Why is there a perception of difficulty? The next step is to consider if this *must* be the case. If not, how can words change the level of difficulty? Each of us owns our perception of difficulty. Leaders should be particularly careful not to place their assumed difficulty onto others.

STORY: TERMINATING TALKS

I have been in leadership positions that required terminating other leaders and employees. As I grew as a leader, these conversations became easier. The reason they became easier reflects how I framed them, to myself and to the other person. Initially, I came to the conversation carrying the heavy weight of responsibility for the information discussed. Once I became a better leader and consistently clarified expectations, I came to termination conversations with a different perception. If a termination was necessary, it reflected a series of choices the person being terminated had made. My responsibility, as well as my choice, was in keeping expectations clear and providing direct feedback at regular intervals. The actual termination conversation was the culmination of the individual's choices and my responsibility was still to provide clarity. I was careful to choose words that aligned with my intentions, which in this case was to hold the team equally accountable to expectations. Ultimately, the other person understood that he or she owned the outcome of this termination conversation.

One of the more notable books and workshops on handling difficult conversations is *Crucial Conversations* by Patterson et al. The main premise is that creating good dialogue is essential to holding crucial conversations. The first step is to focus on your intention and "start with your heart." The book offers a "do it yourself assessment" to better understand your style under stress. The real focus is on how to build better dialogue by making any space safe for discussion. There is a great chapter on leveraging stories; both the ones you tell yourself and the ones you may need to hear differently. There are tips for improving listening skills and asking clarifying questions (Patterson, 2012).

One of the most basic ways to ensure you are owning your intent in any given conversation is to maintain a focus in speaking only from your heart and values. So often conversations at work and with our loved ones are heavily laden with "you" statements. This creates a lack of ownership, as well as the potential for blame. It also sets you up for conversing on the foundation of assumptions. If you flip this and speak primarily from your own perspective, you will indeed present more ownership of your position.

Common conflict guidance suggests that you primarily speak about how something or someone, or their words, have made you *feel*. For example, "You are such a slob; I can't believe you can't just clean your dishes after you use them." This is better replaced with, "It makes me feel unsettled, and as though I need to do something, when I return home to your pile of dirty dishes. I know this relates to my own sense of cleanliness and efficiency. And I wonder how we might strike a win-win." With this approach, you are owning only your part of the conflict and not making any assumptions or laying any blame on the other person. The chances for constructive dialogue and resolution increase, and the probability of unnecessary emotion decreases.

Of interest to me has always been the conversations that spark from customer service shortcomings. Some hold as a tenet that the customer is always right. It serves us well to start personal conversations with that assumption as well. Holding this assumption leads to careful consideration – what went wrong, why did it go wrong, how can we prevent it from going wrong in the future, what was the impact of this error, and how can I remedy the situation? These are all good considerations. Holding this assumption also prevents applying any blame to the customer.

Again, this requires "I" statements as opposed to referring to "you" or the other person. Each of us has found ourselves in a situation when a service is not as expected. The best case scenario is that the person who you share this information with owns the outcome, regardless of whether they were personally responsible for it. Passing the blame serves no purpose. The customer rarely needs to hear what he should have done or what his role in the shortcoming may have been. Making statements such as, "You were supposed to order before 10 a.m." or "If you said you wanted the steak; you sure didn't say it loud enough" doesn't help anybody. It does help contribute to frustration.

These conversations require the use of the words "I" or "we" and other words that represent sorrow, action, regret, concern, being of service, and proactive or future terms. Avoid words related to blame, denial, hopelessness, lack of knowledge, or indifference. These words serve no purpose for the intent of making the situation right. The only purpose they would serve would be to represent the person delivering the message as lacking ownership or true concern for the issue.

New words for the above examples:

1. Instead of "You were supposed to order before 10 a.m." consider saying, "I am sorry our information was unclear. We only accept orders placed before 10 a.m., here is what we can do…"

2. Instead of "If you said you wanted the steak; you sure didn't say it loud enough," consider saying "I apologize for not hearing you properly. I will get a steak right out to you."

Constructive Criticism — Not Just at Work

Constructive criticism can be tricky and is incredibly dependent on one's intent and the mindset of the receiver of the criticism. Some people's levels of self-esteem keep them on high alert for criticism. They perceive criticism in the most benign messages. If they are in a place of defensiveness, they may hear criticism even when that is not the intent. While we are not responsible for the space in which the receiver finds him or herself, we should consider what we know about the person. This is not to cloud intent or to suggest a reliance on assumptions. The suggestion is meant only as additional fodder for consideration when choosing words.

My husband and I can count on both hands the number of times we have raised our voices to our children. However, they went through a phase in their teens when during a normal discussion they might blurt out, "Please stop yelling at me." This has always confused us, as we were not yelling. Eventually, we came to understand that it reflected the space the child was in while receiving the information of the discussion. The real point is that people carry their own history, their perception of that history, and as such, their own perspectives. This has great influence over a person's mental state before, during or after an interaction with another person. Therefore, choosing words carefully in sensitive conversations is critical.

I have found myself in conversations where I need to remind myself that the other person is currently the equivalent of an injured bird due to his personal circumstances. I must take extra care to not provide additional hurt. My words must be reflective of my intent and my values.

Angry Words

I have travelled a lot for business over the last 10 years, which of course means I have had my share of canceled flights and long delays. I have also witnessed others handle these same challenges. Often, cancellations or even changes in travel plans tend to bring out the worst in people.

Here are a few sayings that might pop into your head in such a situation:

- The squeaky wheel gets the grease.
- The early bird gets the worm.
- You catch more flies with honey than vinegar.
- Handle with kid gloves.
- Kill them with kindness.

The only times I have seen an approach that is full of anger and venom work is when the receiver has given up due to exasperation. While I wish to commiserate with both parties I am observing, it is often hard not to feel that the angry person might choose better words. A lot of the times the same goes for the airline attendant.

An angry approach is typically also accusatory. What is interesting about this is that rarely is the attendant responsible for the delay or cancellation. Imagine now an interaction with lots of accusations, expletives, and condescension – you have heard this interaction before. What purpose does this approach serve?

POTENTIAL POSITIVES:

- The customer blows off steam and somehow "feels" better.
- The customer feels in control.

POTENTIAL NEGATIVES:

- The attendant feels even more poorly for the effect the cancellation or delay has on the customers.
- The attendant feels powerless.
- The attendant feels verbally abused.
- The attendant may become defensive.

- The customer has shown an ugly side of him or herself.
- Observers are embarrassed for the customer's outrage.
- Observers feel poorly for the attendant.

"Shit happens" is a truism. When it does, know the power of your words and use them for the good of all. I assure you, it serves no purpose to denigrate another with your words. This will not make you feel better and will make you look like a jerk. Rise above the inconvenience and choose words that represent your values and offer a win-win.

Chapter Wrap

Most of us spend at least a third of each weekday at work. This is a considerable amount of time and an enormous opportunity to contribute. Whether you are an employee or leader, what you do and say daily makes an impact. Your word choices impact coworkers, your team, your boss, or your customers. It is beneficial to assess how well your personal values align with your organization's values. People who are fortunate to work in an environment where their personal values align with the company values are well positioned to feel fulfilled by their work. Values are the foundation for choosing the best words in any given circumstance – whether you are the boss or the employee. Regardless of your role at work, words matter.

Words impact coworkers and customers as much as they do our loved ones and everyone in between. They are an expression of our true selves. Nowadays, we have more options than just words for expressing ourselves. I *heart* that you have come this far in discovering how, why, and when you choose certain words. This leads me to ask you this: How does technology challenge your word choices? We will explore this in the next chapter.

Chapter FIVE

WORDS THAT CONNECT US IN OTHER MEDIUMS

When our kids were in the ninth grade, they told us stories of friends ending their relationships via text. We discussed this extensively as they both had just received cell phones. We asked each of them how they would feel if this happened to them and reviewed the value in being more sensitive and direct. Choosing the right time, setting, and words were part of our conversation.

Sure enough, our son broke up with his girlfriend six months later by text. A more extensive conversation followed. We reviewed how this may have made him feel had the tables been turned. We talked about his intention – it was not to hurt her, but it was to break up as easily as possible. We evaluated values, such as communicating honestly and directly, treating others kindly, owning actions and words. He had the opinion that this was the kindest way to end the relationship and that a face-to-face conversation would have been harder for them both. He agreed that he would not have appreciated such a text. "Do unto others as you would have them do unto you" won him over. He spoke to her the very next day.

This 21st century version of the "Dear John" letter may work for some people. Written words do not have the benefit of the emotion and intent represented in facial expressions and body language.

When situations like this are handled in person, the "dumpee" can see if this is hard for the "dumper," if they are struggling for the words, and if they care about what they are saying. In person, there is a dialogue, not simply an exchange of words. In this case, the potential exists for the exchange to be heart to heart.

This may remind some of you of the 2008 *Sex and the City* episode when Berger breaks up with Carrie on a Post-it Note. I wanted to refresh my memory and found a great reference in *Vogue Magazine*. Emma Specter suggests the following, "Now we live in the age of Tinder and Hinge, when it's possible to exchange witty banter with a potential partner without ever leaving your room. Given the ever-increasing indignities of dating via apps and text, Berger's sad Post-it Note actually feels—dare I say it?—borderline romantic." She goes on to offer, "Berger actually took the time to write words on paper and leave them for his girlfriend (or, to be more accurate, ex-girlfriend) to find. Cowardly, sure, but compared to a "hey sry dont think i can do this :(" text received at 4 a.m., it's practically a carefully composed love letter from John Adams to his wife Abigail." (Specter, 2019).

As we compress our language into fewer characters and words, the need to choose the right ones amplifies. Additionally, these formats can last in cyberspace forever. The shift from speaking words to expressing them through technology mediums grows exponentially each year. Even if you intend to abbreviate your words, they should still come from your heart and represent your intention.

Email and Text

Emails and texts require the same considerations as spoken words. The first choice you need to make is which of these formats serves you best for a particular message. These days, both are used for personal and professional communication. You could text your grandmother sweet heart and hug emojis and in the next moment ask your coworker when she will send the report you need. Texting in the wrong window and sending your message to the wrong person is much more likely than emailing the wrong recipient. The most common email faux pas is hitting "reply all" with a message intended only for the sender. These challenges support the need to slow down, reflect on your intent, and choose your format and words wisely. Here are some considerations.

- Does the text or email represent your intention?
- Are you clear about the purpose this communication serves?
- Have you chosen the appropriate format – email or text?
- Would a conversation be better?

There are some socially correct conventions for email and text. They relate more to how you use words and less to the word choice. Consider all that has come before in this book for your word choices. Know your company's policy on text and email usage. Here are common conventions and a few of my own recommendations. Some of them may be more appropriate for professional messages, but worth considering in your personal interactions as well.

- Minimize use of ALL CAPS – what you write in all caps will BE READ AS YELLING. This only applies to email, as text messages do not allow for font changes (size, bold, underline or italics) and CAPS is the only way to emphasize a point. Instead of CAPS in an email, choose to use bold, underlined or italicized words for impact.
- Keep Texts under 200 characters – 100 is even better, otherwise you have a missive that may be better as a conversation or an email.
- If you volley an email back and forth twice, consider picking up the phone. This usually indicates one of the two parties needs more information or that a deeper conversation will help. The same applies to a string of texts.
- When a text or email rubs you the wrong way, plan to speak in

person or at least by phone. Conflict is sometimes perceived due to misunderstanding the intent of a message.

- Choose "reply all" very carefully – only when others truly need to hear your response.

- CC (carbon copy) and BCC (blind carbon copy) appropriately – these two features speak to accountability. Simply choosing how someone is addressed on an email communicates something, even without words. Decide if the words you send to the main audience require the knowledge of those you wish to CC or BCC. CC those you wish to be in the loop, but who are not expected to respond. BCC those you wish to be in the loop, but do not want the other recipients to know they are in the loop. Interestingly, some employers promote this type of back door accountability and others discourage any use of BCC. Using BCC can equate to "tattling" at work.

- Choose your "subject line" words very carefully, they impact the reader's interest and urgency. I appreciate the following prompts in the subject line: *URGENT, PLS REVIEW BY MONDAY, NEEDS APPROVAL* (and yes, the words are in all caps intentionally).

- In a few pages, I address salutations and signing off or closing. These standards apply to email as well.

- Keep your words to a minimum and in bullet form if providing specific details.

- When you know you are sending an email that is apt to be contentious, sit on it. Give yourself time to review and ask yourself: *What is my intention? What purpose does this email serve?*

Social Media

Time spent on social media has grown steadily since 2012. In 2019, the average time spent on social media worldwide was 144 minutes a day. That equates to 6 years and 8 months in a lifetime! This is up by **one hour** a day, or 62.5 percent over 2012. North American usage falls in the middle of the use by continent. South America's usage is highest, then Africa, North America, Asia/Oceania, and Europe (Average Daily Time on Social Media, 2020).

It is likely that the COVID-19 pandemic boosted these numbers significantly. It is hard to imagine what the "shelter-in-place" requirements around the world would have been like with no Internet, no social media, no email or text, and no Zoom! Connections with loved ones is infinitely easier with Internet access and all the related tools. I suspect many older adults have learned skills they did not expect to need in their lifetimes.

Social media has become a standard part of politics, news consumption, and daily human interaction. According to the World Economic Forum, Gen Z is the first generation that does not know the world without the Internet. Baby Boomers rank last in social media usage followed by Gen X, then Millennials. Gen Z leads the way in utilizing all the internet has to offer them socially (Visual Capitalist, 2019).

In 2017, Twitter went from 140 to 280 words per post. The most common length of a tweet before this change was 34 characters. Now that the limit is 280 characters, the most common length of a tweet is 33 characters. Historically, only 9 percent of tweets hit Twitter's 140-character limit, now only 1 percent hit 140. Twitter's doubling of character count from 140 to 280 had little impact on length of tweets (Perez, 2018). Instead, threads – or strings of tweets – have become increasingly popular.

This is all very curious. Why would we use even fewer, or just as few, when given more characters per post? Why the popularity of threads? Are several, more brief statements more effective than fewer but longer ones? I do not have these answers and will continue to watch these trends in how we express ourselves publicly as well as how we consume social media. Regardless of why we are trending in this direction, the fact remains that we are choosing to express ourselves in fewer words and this requires careful consideration of those few words.

During an election year in the United States, more and more politicians are adopting tweets as their way to reach a broad audience, as well as banter with each other. Many advertise or spread their campaign messages via Facebook and Instagram. At the same time, caution is advised in determining what is real or fake on social media platforms. Alarmingly, since January 2017, the United States has learned of most official changes to government leadership and policy through "presidential tweets."

Typically, Instagram posts are pictures, articles or memes. LinkedIn posts are articles, brief thoughts, and occasionally memes all geared toward the work environment. Facebook is a mixture of all – articles, memes, pictures, missives, and personal thoughts. Each of these forums has unspoken, generally accepted guidelines for usage. Most organizations, universities, public entities also provide their teams with guidelines. Sometimes the choice of medium is based on "staying power" or visibility. For example, Facebook and Instagram posts last forever, but content shared in "stories" and Snapchats are not automatically saved. I will leave it to you to research more on your preferred platform.

The bottom line is that as we express ourselves in such abbreviated forms, our word choices are exponentially more important. Sometimes we express ourselves without even using words. We can post an emoji or simply give a thumbs up or heart to imply liking a post or comment. All previous suggestions for choosing words apply.

REFLECTION

Think back to your last social media interactions and consider the following:

1. What is your true intention for your tweet, Facebook post, Instagram picture?
2. How well does this intention align with your values?
3. How would a Facebook interaction be different in person? Would you say the same things?
4. Does your comment matter? To whom does it matter?
5. Is your intent solely to entertain?
6. Are you confident that your post or comment will not offend another being? Is offense your intent?
7. Are there different words that would serve your intent better?
8. Have you used too few words to have the impact you intended?

Thank You Notes

The art of note writing may be waning but carries a great impact. The most important thing about writing any card is that the sentiment is authentic. The second most important thing is that it is specific.

Sometimes it feels like the art of the handwritten, thank you note is evaporating. The more it shrinks, the more two things happen: 1) The recipient is even more surprised and potentially overjoyed and 2) The notes sent to homes are of even greater value. Earlier I mentioned a tip on how to encourage yourself to send notes routinely. Here, I would like to discuss the content of the notes. The words you choose influence the intended outcome in sending the note.

ACTIVITY

Read the following two notes and circle any words that may have an impact on Tina. Answer these questions:

1. Which note sounds more authentic? Why?
2. Which is more specific?
3. What difference does the specificity make?

Dear Tina,

Your patient in room 205 last week was very pleased with his care. I'm glad you have settled into your role on the team. Many thanks, Susan

Dear Tina,

Today, I heard from one of our patients about the wonderful care you provided to him. He specifically mentioned how well you anticipated his needs and how clear you were in establishing expectations for the day. I very much appreciate how you live our value of providing excellent service. You are a valuable member of the team. I appreciate you!

Thanks for the difference you make every day,

Susan

Love Notes

When is the last time you sent a note from your heart to the heart of another person? That is a love note. They come in all shapes and sizes and hopefully when least expected. We all need to send and receive more of them. Here is why:

- They last forever and can be reviewed as often as the recipient desires.
- You can take your time and truly contemplate your word choices.
- The perception that writing one is a greater effort (than calling or texting) adds to the perceived value of the note.

- It feels so good to hold the words from someone's heart in your hand.

I had the honor of coaching a world-class note writer, Todd Hendricks. Todd has routinely sent me meaningful handwritten notes. They are often funny, always heartfelt, and never expected. They brighten my day every time one resurfaces in my office. When we were working closely in his town, he periodically sent notes to my kids thanking them for "sharing me" and telling them great things about the work I do. In doing so, he reinforced the value of such notes to my kids. This small act of kindness goes such a long way for the cost of some time and a stamp. I challenge you to send a note from your heart to the heart of another before you finish reading this book.

Sympathy Cards

Expressing sympathy is not as well practiced as expressing gratitude. This is a good thing if there is less to sympathize with, but it may require even more contemplation. The more difficult an action feels, the less likely we are to do it. Hallmark and others do a good job capturing the basic sentiments, thereby lessening the effort. However, crafting your own message of sympathy is decidedly more authentic and will mean more to the recipient. At the very least, you have an opportunity to personalize the greeting card message with a few of your own heartfelt words of support.

In expressing sympathy, the same suggestion to be specific applies. Defining a few keywords that you can weave into most expressions of sympathy will make the effort easier.

If my intention in writing a sympathy card is typically to acknowledge loss and provide support, I might craft a couple of lines that represent my voice. For example, I may find it comfortable to weave in, "I am so sorry to hear of the passing of _____.... *Then write something personal…* I hope that you and your family are finding the courage you need in this difficult time. Please know that I am here for you." See Chapter Three's section on words for those who are grieving for more keywords.

Birthday Cards

I have two words to emphasize with birthday cards: Send them! In the technology world we live in today, a handful of birthday cards annually might be your most meaningful mail. It is so easy to see a prompt on Facebook or LinkedIn that today is someone's birthday and to quickly shoot them a message. While that might be heartfelt and feel like a good connection, it by no means replaces the hand-written card in your mailbox. Again, greeting card producers provide a plethora of options as a starting place for your personalized message. Whether you go the route of a pre-formulated message, you can ensure that your connection is personal and meets the intent of honoring the recipient. The words to choose for such a card should be all about the recipient. Any sort of acknowledgment of them and their attributes is always appropriate for this annual celebration.

If you desire a more environmentally-conscious option, choose e-cards that you can customize. This option does not have the same impact as the card received at home, but you and the recipient may have fun with this. You can customize with pictures and music in many cases.

ACTIVITY

Score yourself on the following by marking one point for each card sent
In the past year, I sent the following cards. Be sure to note the number of cards
sent for each occasion in the box.

[ ] Birthdays (friends and family)

[ ] Sympathy

[ ] Thank you (for your birthday gifts, holiday gifts, for an act of
kindness)

[ ] Love Notes (thinking of you, or the 'just cuz note)

[ ] Holiday celebration

[ ] Other

Total your score. Note below to whom and for what occasion you might
send cards in the coming 12 months that would take your score beyond 12.
Twelve is one card a month. I bet you have either 12 friends and family members or 12 distinct events that might warrant a hand-written acknowledge-
ment in the coming year.

I will send a note to:

1.

2.

3.

4.

5.

6.

I will send a card for the following occasions:

7.

8.

9.

10.

11.

12.

This note was sent to my colleague, Lisa Solis Delong. It touched Lisa deeply to know that a busy Chief Nursing Officer took the time (in April of 2020 during peak pandemic days) to write her a personal note. It thrills me to read that Lisa's *words* are an inspiration to this leader.

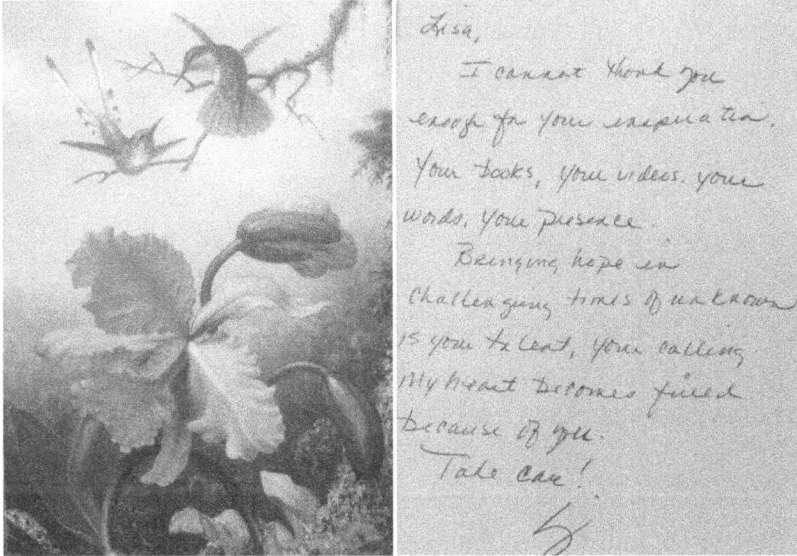

Salutations and Closing

For the longest time in my work life, I signed off emails with, "Live your purpose, Terre." I began to think this might be too direct, similar to "Have a great day," but an even taller order. After many years of using this phrase, I considered if my personal value of living my purpose was something to suggest to others. I also weighed how I value not being too direct. The combination of these thoughts led me to drop this sign off, at least for a while. These days, I find it appropriate to end with "Stay well, Terre." I will use this for as long as it feels right. Some of the more common and generically acceptable sign offs are: Warm regards, all the best, best, sincerely, and warmly.

I propose these considerations:

- Consider your audience
- Consider the context (work or personal)
- Consider your values and intention
- Consider your desired impact

After making these considerations, choose wisely. In today's world, individuality is usually acceptable and encouraged. Choose words that serve you and connect you to others as you desire. These words may be your "last word flag."

Chapter Wrap

I left a decorative wooden block with the words "Call Mom" in my son's dorm room as we settled him in freshman year. He heeded it sparingly. I cherish every time he does pick up the phone and I have learned to appreciate the occasional Snapchat, Instagram story, text, or even Facebook tag to a message I post.

Social media's reduction in characters to communicate should not reduce your character – or intent. Stay true to yourself in all mediums and know when a face-to-face conversation is warranted. Be diligent about using the best medium for your message. Put as much consideration into your word choices for a tweet, text, email and note card as you would in a face-to-face conversation. If you suspect the intent of your message has gotten lost as a result of the medium or brevity, connect differently. Do not let emojis limit your expression and ability to connect with another. Periodically, seek feedback and clarity when you suspect technology or social media use may not be representing the true you. Don't be afraid to take a break and connect through a handwritten note or a phone call.

We live in a time with seemingly endless ways to connect. We get to choose from a myriad of mediums to express ourselves, almost minute by minute. In every platform choice, words matter.

"One should therefore not rely on mere words, but everywhere search for the intention behind them." (121)

EDWARD CONZE, BUDDHIST SCRIPTURES

Chapter SIX

WORDS THAT CONNECT US WITH THE UNIVERSE AND SPIRIT

A great deal of this book has explored the words we send out into the world. As we conclude this exploration, I want to walk with you through the origin of our words as they relate to our spiritual practice and deeper belief structures. I anticipate and honor that every reader has a different perspective on spirituality. I use "Universe" as a receptacle for a myriad of beliefs and paradigms that speak to personal and collective spirituality. I encourage you to wade into this chapter with compassion and curiosity, taking into account that we are all capable of greeting every situation with loving kindness and for many of us, this is rooted in our core belief system (as discussed in previous chapters). It has long-stopped surprising me that when I meet especially effective communicators, they often have some sort of personal spiritual practice or mode of exploration that directly or indirectly informs their words choices. It is my hope that we continue to evolve as a species through our ability to communicate.

I attended Catholic schools most of my life, even a Jesuit University. I was baptized Lutheran. I recall my parents dressing us up for holiday church services as a child, but little else about the Lutheran religion. I attended Mass regularly during my school years. When I was 17, I became interested in all world religions. I recall announcing to my parents that I wanted to convert to Judaism. My study of world religions opened my eyes to the various ways in which people connect themselves to a higher power.

I took two years of Latin during my studies at Loyola University. My favorite part of knowing this lost language was attending Mass in Latin. The words were intentional, melodic, and enhanced the ritual. I discovered two of my favorites on the Epic Pew Website (Vennet, 2015). You might read these Latin sentences aloud.

Gloria Patri, et filio, et spiritui sancto (Glow-ree-ah-pah-tree-eht-fee-lee-oh-eht-speer-it-too-e-san-ktoe) = Glory be to the Father, and to the Son, and to the Holy Spirit

Agnus dei, qui tolis peccata mundi (Ahn-use-day-e-qwee-tow-lease-peck-ah-tah-moon-dee) = Lamb of God, who takes away the sins of the world

There is so much to gain from spiritual practices. This overview is meant to set the context for communication with that which is greater than us.

I invite you to consider what you might be transmitting from your heart and how your word choices might impact your transmission. There are various ways people around the world connect with the universe. Some do so through their faith in a deity. Others connect through their own practice and may invoke goddesses, gods, God, their own guides, Divine Spirit, healing energies – the options are as diverse as the individuals on this planet. The common thread is intention. I will overview four conduits for setting and expressing intention as frameworks for exploring the significance of the words when connecting to the universe.

> "Meditation is all about the pursuit of nothingness."
>
> HUGH JACKMAN

Meditation

Sometimes the voice in our head is our way of connecting with the universe. It can take on many forms. In meditation, one works to quiet the internal voice and to open space for just being. It is a sacred time for hearing and accepting all that the universe is providing. Meditation can be a spiritual practice. It can provide physical relaxation with a focus on the body and breath. There are many types of meditation and related benefits. Humans have practiced meditation for thousands of years. In its simplest form, it serves the purpose of regulating and monitoring one's attention, thereby cultivating wellbeing. A quick search on the Internet will reveal an abundance of books, videos, and articles related to meditation. Some are specifically for beginners and others offer guidance to integrating Buddhist wisdom or maximizing performance (such as better sleep, more motivation, less stress, more productivity). Videos provide guided meditation that incorporates breathing and attention to one's body. Prior to slipping into a meditative state, one might set an intention for this time spent in quiet contemplation. I am by no means a meditation expert. My experience and research lead me to believe that since one point is to quiet the voice in my head, I only choose a few words. I may choose a mantra to keep my focus aligned. I might set an intention prior to starting my meditation. A clear intention helps guide my breath and the energy I am giving and receiving. I may choose words such as:

- I am open to the light that comes to me with each breath.
- Each breath fills me with abundance, each exhale expresses my gratitude.
- My body is my vessel for receiving and providing love.
- I am love.

Reflection and Gratitude

A daily practice of quiet reflection often leads to a sense of gratitude and acknowledgment – acknowledgment of what the universe needs from you and what you intend your contribution to be, even just for that day. Centering oneself in a place of gratitude helps to frame the voice in your head. An example would be taking three deep breaths before sliding out of bed in the morning and contemplating those things for which you are grateful. During the COVID-19 pandemic, I routinely awoke and thought of the rest and comfort I had enjoyed during the night. I proceeded to ask the Divine Spirit to provide rest to all caregivers who were lacking sleep and comfort to those without roofs over their heads and clean bedding. Keeping a gratitude journal is an impactful habit that provides mounting evidence to counter any negativity the voice in your head might suggest. Gratitude journals are useful for documenting, and thereby expressing, one's intentions. Journal apps such as DayOne can also serve this purpose.

Mealtime is another opportunity for expressing gratitude. As a child, I recall this common prayer at most every family table.

> *Bless us, oh Lord,*
> *and these thy gifts which*
> *we are about to receive from thy bounty,*
> *through Christ, Our Lord.*
> *Amen.*

I have heard these words mumbled, spoken at breakneck speed, and even slurred. I do not recall any true connection between the words and my gratitude for the meal in front of me. I would venture to say, my expression in this prayer had more to do with compliance than appreciation.

Do you chant rote words that served you in your youth? Do they still serve you? Is your gratitude expressed in a way that benefits the

greater good, or specific individuals? You may choose to acknowledge all those who made your meal possible, those who picked and
cleaned the vegetables, those who caught the fish, or even the actual
fish. You may choose to send nurturing words of love to those less
fortunate, who might be missing a meal. Either way, I challenge you
to consider if the words you currently choose serve your intention
and if choosing different ones might benefit others in this world.

Appreciation is born out of awareness and leads to even more awareness. When in quiet contemplation, you might reflect on your dwell-
ing, nutrition, work, or health. If your approach is one of appreciation,
you will find a deeper awareness of what you are contemplating in
the first place. Let us pretend you are having a walk in the neighborhood, quietly reflecting, and you become aware of a large oak tree
with brilliant gold leaves. You pause to appreciate the color. In doing
so, you become aware of how large the tree is and ponder how long
it has been standing. This may lead you to be grateful for the shade it
has provided for so many years and the beauty of the leaves.

This is a great time to connect the words in your head to your values. Choosing specific words to clarify your gratitude is important and
will influence the energy you create. If I take the same walk (allegedly
to clear my mind) routinely, and do not put words to my observations,
I am missing an opportunity to feel and express gratitude. Other
words in my head may be distracting me from true awareness and
therefore appreciation. This might all sound like "squirrel!" or a dis-
traction. Reflection time in nature presents a win-win-win. You take
time to align the voice in your head with your intentions, you make
observations that trigger your gratitude, and you create positive
energy when you express that gratitude back into the universe. Let
us work through an example. I have highlighted intentional word
choices.

I am walking in my neighborhood, contemplating an upcoming
call I have with a client. I am considering how prepared I am and
what I recall from our last session.

I hear the voice say, *I am not sure Sharon likes me or my style.* I decide to explore that thought.

Where did that come from? What did Sharon do or say that caused me to **think** *that?*

Answer: *Nothing, that is not a* **valuable** *thought. I am* **confident** *in my* **abilities** *and if I sense any disconnect, I will inquire in the moment. I am a* **skillful** *coach.*

Then I think, *How can I* **serve** *Sharon well today?*

Answer: *I will be* **present** *and not worry about when I will pack for our trip. Whoa, where did that come from? I have* **plenty of time** *to pack and need not worry at all. I am* **thankful** *for the timing of our call.*

Which leads me to think, *What else am I* **thankful** *for?*

Answer: **Wow!** *Look at those oak leaves! Were they that* **bright** *last fall? This tree is* **amazing**. *I* **appreciate** *its many years of* **providing** *great fall colors and* **abundant** *shade. I* **am ready** *to get back to the office and to speak with Sharon.*

> "I used to believe that prayer changes things but now I know that prayer changes us and we change things."
>
> MOTHER THERESA

Prayer

Great Mystery,
teach me how to trust
my heart,
my mind,
my intuition,
my inner knowing,
the senses of my body,
the blessings of my spirit.

Teach me to trust these things
so that I may enter my Sacred Space
and love beyond my fear,
and thus Walk in Balance
with the passing of each glorious Sun.
~Lakota Prayer

Praying involves acknowledgment of blessings and invokes gratitude. Praying can be a place of contemplation and the assertion of positive energy. Praying can be a direct request to a deity depending on one's religious beliefs. Praying might be like talking to your best friend. Some people find solace in this daily connection. Although this is a one-way conversation, a response may be in a future sign, a happening, or as the voice in your head.

The words "prayer" and "pray" mean different things to people around the world, even in my family. I like to consider the evolution of prayer, at least on an individual basis. You might be crystal clear about setting an intention in the universe and not associate this action with "praying." You might express gratitude in a variety of ways throughout the day and not once find yourself in "prayer." The world's spiritual traditions, religious practices and even mythology all provide opportunities for exploring your own evolution of prayer.

> "Worrying is praying for what you don't want."
> JRR TOLKIEN

Regardless of how you choose to connect and reflect, or to whom you direct your communication, these times of contemplation also necessitate carefully chosen words. Here are some questions to contemplate:

1. Do your words in prayer represent your intent and what you

value? For instance, are you grateful without judgment, quali-
fication, or minimization?

2. What is the lens through which you identify your gratitude?
   Is it in relation to others, or to your desires, or to the greater
   universe?

3. Do your prayers and reflections serve to reinforce your values,
   to take you beyond your perceived limitations?

4. Are there any words you use that compromise or denigrate
   your contribution?

5. What portion of your thoughts and prayers involve others and
   what part is all you?

These are all good questions for assessing the power of the words
you are choosing. Are there better words that would more overtly
represent your values and intention for a time of prayer, meditation
or reflection? These times lay the foundation for your daily inner
voice, which you may hear into the night. How well you frame these
thoughts affects your continued inner dialogue. Using different
words may simply mean being more specific.

ACTIVITY

Recall the last time you held space for a form of quiet contemplation.
Think of the three main thoughts you focused on and note them below in the
first column. Then, tease out the specific keywords you recall saying or thinking and place them in the second column. In the third column, identify what
your intent was and note in the fourth column if you met your intent with the
words you chose. Lastly, craft some words that may serve you better or bring
more clarity to your intentions.

Why use a chart? You might be thinking, "I didn't expect to see a chart in
this section!" We all process differently and even the "chart-adverse" among
us might find it helpful to take a linear look at how we craft thoughts into words.

Remember: If you are looking for guidance you must be specific! Two
examples are provided.

Thought	Keywords or Phrases Used	Intent	Did words match intent? Yes/No	Better words to incorporate
EX: I prayed for the safety of the firefighters in the recent California fires.	*Keep them safe, meet their needs for rest and nutrition*	*To express my gratitude for their work and provide support for them*	*Not entirely*	*I am **grateful** for all of the firefighters.* *May they know their worth.* *I pray their needs are being met – lots of rest, hydration and nutrition.*
EX: I asked the Divine Spirit to help me with an upcoming conversation with a coworker.	*I **think** I am prepared. I know I **have to** do this. I'm going to **need** all the **help** I can get.*	*To seek to understand that I am on the right track*	*NO*	*What more do I need to be fully prepared? What will be the benefit of this conversation (that I may be grateful for)?* *How can I bring my true self to this conversation?*
1.				
2.				
3.				

Plants and Animals

As humans become increasingly concerned about the health of our planet, we are learning more about our connection to all living things. There is a plethora of literature that confirms the ability of plants and animals to communicate. Our universe is made up of living systems. Ecological studies continue to explore how complex ecosystems communicate. Research also suggests that indigenous people from all continents understood/understand this, as is represented in their spiritual practices.

It is thrilling to read mainstream articles about the increased attention by the scientific community to better understand what the earliest inhabitants of our earth seemed to know. "Why Scientists Are Starting to Care About Cultures That Talk to Whales," an article by Krista Langlois in the *Smithsonian Magazine*, is one such example. Thankfully, enough humans are connecting with their inherent ability to listen and learn from other species that we can no longer ignore communication on this level. Langlois explains how Artic natives' centuries of communication with whales challenges common Western beliefs. Studies such as this bring the superiority of senses and skills of humans into question. It also leads to contemplation of our interconnectedness and therefore reliance on the intelligence of other species. It seems we are well overdue for validating the effectiveness of this level of communication.

In the book, *Braiding Sweetgrass: Indigenous Wisdom, Scientific Knowledge, and the Teaching of Plants*, Robin Wall Kimmerer beautifully explains how indigenous languages have long observed a grammar of animacy. Plants, animals, rocks, mountains, water, and even places are considered animate. "Beings that are imbued with spirit, our secret medicines, our songs, drums, and even stories, are all animate," she writes. Her distillation of the difference in how indigenous people honor plants and animals boils down to this statement, "The arrogance of English is that the only way to be animate, to be worthy of respect and moral concern, is to be human." (Kimmerer, 2015).

I stumbled across Sarah Bowen, by reading an article she wrote for *Spirituality and Health* magazine. The title caught my eye, "How I Became an Animal Chaplain." I reached out to her to learn more about things her animal advocacy taught her that we all should know.

Sarah teaches at One Spirit Interfaith Seminary in New York City. Thirty different religions are represented in her classes. She also published, *Spiritual Rebel: A Positively Addictive Guide to Finding Deeper Perspective and Higher Purpose* (Bowen, 2019). While regarding her work and speaking to her, it occurred to me that she is a word expert herself, particularly in the areas of spirituality and inter-species.

At the end of her book, Sarah offers 175 words for "God" – and she is still counting. She refers to these as pointer words and provides a compelling argument for how words simply "point" us toward a person, place, or thing. Through stories, she illustrates how words are our guideposts and that oftentimes words fall short of representing everyone's definition or understanding of the subject the word signifies. "God" is a perfect example of this. She also uses multiple words for invocation to increase inclusivity. She shares how inclusivity can go beyond gender, race, ethnicity, and other categorizations to extend to all species. She invokes "interbeingness," which was coined by Thich Nhat Hanh, as well as "otherkind," and "animalkind." She leverages Lisa Kemmerer's "anymal" and David Abram's "more-than-human world." Sarah has also coined the word "spiritualtarian" to describe people who endeavor to align each one of their choices with their spiritual values.

Sarah has provided tips on inter-species meditation below. While her specialty involves cats, predominantly domestic ones, she has meditated with the sacred white lions of Timbavati. She speaks of the benefits to both parties, especially the ability for humans to increase their compassion beyond the construct of human exceptionalism. Listening to her summarize the experiences and the effect such interactions can have in the world made me quite hopeful for our species.

REFLECTION: **Inter-species Mindfulness Practices from** *Spiritual Rebel: A Positively Addictive Guide to Finding Deeper Perspective and Higher Purpose*:

Puppy dog eyes: When your dog is calm and blissed-out, try gazing into its eyes for a few moments. Takefumi Kikusui (an animal behaviorist at Azabu University in Japan) examined the impact of eye contact in dogs and their human companions. He found that with sustained gazing, oxytocin levels increased in both the dog and the human. "Oxytocin is a hormone associated with trust and maternal bonding. It increases when you're close to someone you love and gives you that warm fuzzy feeling." Gaze into the deep mystery that lives within the eyes of your canine companion, breathing slowly in and out.

Cat gazing: Many cats can find staring a challenge, so instead of staring in their eyes, just sit quietly nearby. Become aware of your cat's furry body rising and lowering. From this awareness, tune into your cat's breaths. Matching your inhales and exhales, become a melded being, resting in your breath.

Not-so-squirrely mind: Squirrels are remarkably attuned to human actions, so it's best to stand still and gaze at the squirrel just past its body. Often, it will take the same pose, silently starring back. Notice how it feels to connect in stillness with a different species outside of your home.

Forest bathing: Head to somewhere green. Then slowly tune in to the flow of life force within yourself. Soften your eyes. Think about the expansiveness of the Earth. Start to wander. Bathe your senses. What do you see? Smell? Hear? How does the ground feel? How does the air taste? Notice the connections. Leaves are parts of trees, but whole within themselves. Consider cycles in progress around you: plants live, die, become part of the soil from which they sprouted. Reflect. After your wander, journal about any meaningful moments of connection.

Cosmic connection: Breathe in and out slowly, contemplating how far "up" is. Consider these ideas: You are a tiny part of a massive galaxy, one of over one hundred billion galaxies, with the nearest 600,000 light years from you. Each year, a thousand tons of Martian rocks rain down on Earth from nearly 34 million miles away. You are one of over seven billion humans among 8.7 million more species of life on Earth. Close your eyes gently, and rest in this vastness for a few moments, then gently open your eyes. Look at your hand, then at your foot. Consider how small you are, one tiny blip in an ever-expanding, increasingly connected universe. Around 10,000 different species of microorganisms call you home. Your body is made up of around 37.2 trillion cells, 2 billion of them in your heart alone. Information is zooming along your nerves at about 250 miles per hour. Consider how large you are: An entire world lives within you.

There are endless options for spiritual practice. It is possible to cultivate a practice regardless of whether you have a religious affiliation or belief. Spiritual practice informs our sense of self, encourages introspection, and builds the patience and awareness that informs the words we choose. These choices allow us to do better. The following reflection may provide inspiration for exploring a spiritual practice. May your practice be unique to your journey and founded on words that serve you well.

REFLECTION

1. How do you relate to animals and plants?
2. Have you ever thanked a tree for the air you breathe?
3. Do you believe your pet understands you? If so, do you choose words that convey kindness and gratitude?
4. Do you routinely include all of Mother Earth in your prayer and reflections? Should you? What words would you choose?

AN IROQUOIS PRAYER

We return thanks to our mother,
the earth, which sustains us.
We return thanks to the rivers and streams,
which supply us with water.
We return thanks to all herbs,
which furnish medicines
for the cure of our diseases.
We return thanks to the corn,
and to her sisters, the beans and squash,
which give us life.
We return thanks to the bushes and trees,
which provide us with fruit.
We return thanks to the wind,
which, moving the air,
has banished diseases.
We return thanks to the moon and the stars,
which have given us their light
when the sun was gone.
We return thanks to our grandfather He-no,
who has given to us his rain.
We return thanks to the sun,
that he has looked upon the earth
with a beneficent eye.
Lastly, we return thanks to the Great Spirit.
in whom is embodied all goodness.
and who directs all things,
for the good of his children.
(Prayer to Mother Earth, 2020)

Chapter Wrap

Polarities exist all around us and inform the cycles of life. When one pole is out of balance, there is a natural swing toward the other pole. This could be the upside or downside of that pole. All poles have inherent positive and negative energy.

What does this have to do with the words you choose to connect with the universe? The right balance is needed for the binaries of beliefs and values. Regardless of your religious beliefs and spiritual practices, we all share this planet. Hopefully, we are all driving toward the greater good. As I write this, there are growing examples of religious beliefs driving ill intent, or harm, to others. Some hate crimes in recent years have ties to religious fundamentalists. These instances are worldwide and not specific to one religion. Lynchings were carried out by people who believed their religion justified crimes against their victims. Hate has been rationalized by doctrine for as long as religion has existed. This knowledge should give us pause to periodically consider how, or if, our religious beliefs align with our values and the good of all. If they are out of alignment, it might be time to reassess what you believe and why.

Another example would be the changing tides in how some religions have treated or accepted gay people. Abolishing conversion therapy, which some religious institutions support as "a step in the right direction," is an example of how a belief may be misaligned. For example, if I had a gay son, I might say, "I value happiness, celebration of self, believe he can achieve anything, and know he is pure joy." These are statement of my values. I might also consider how I believe in my faith and that conversion therapy is the best route for him to truly be himself. This denotes a belief. These two things do not align. I am allowing doctrine to dictate what is best for my son without regard for who he is.

Once we are clear with ourselves, and our place in the cosmic scheme of things, we can be truly present and intentional with how we express ourselves to others.

Why dig deeper? Because the health of humanity and our planet require pure intentions. This starts with how our beliefs inform our values, which dictates our behaviors, and leads to how we express ourselves. Ultimately, all of this plays out in the words we choose when setting intention and in relating to others. Each of us gets to decide not only the specific words, but also to whom we direct the words. Words matter and carry great spiritual power.

"The capacity to learn is a gift. The ability to learn is a skill. The willingness to learn is a choice."

BRIAN HERBERT

Conclusion

My family arrived in Queenstown, New Zealand for a family vacation, in mid-March of 2020 when COVID-19 was rapidly accelerating its global spread. While some of our family returned to the U.S. before travel was restricted, we chose to stay at the family home we were visiting. With us was my husband's 87-year-old aunt who built the home, our daughter and her cousin. We spent most of our time together in "lockdown" as the New Zealand Prime Minister led an extremely focused attack on eliminating the COVID-19 virus.

We listened as the world applauded her efforts. For years to come, I suspect we will read analyses of how world leaders led during this crisis. While it is fresh, I want to share what we witnessed in New Zealand, as it validates the importance of word choices. Prime Minister Jacinda Ardern communicates exceptionally well.

Prime Minister Ardern holds regular press briefings in which she gives clear, definitive direction. She provides data, research, and medical expertise that informs the *why* behind her directives. In every briefing she uses words to express empathy for the challenges of the lockdown, as well as the loss of individual lives. She uses Facebook Live for chats and her team provides updates via WhatsApp. As of March 28, 2020, there have been 19 deaths, or 3.89 deaths per million people in New Zealand. On this same day, the death rate worldwide per million people is 26.4 and in the United States it is 171.67 per million people, or 56,164 individuals (Statista, 2020).

I cannot think of a time when words have mattered more. The words we choose for loved ones far and near. The words we hold onto when we ponder the loss. The lack of words for expressing profound gratitude for all essential workers, including clinicians on the front lines. Just as in wartime, the words of leaders are expected to rally their nations and calm fears. We have chosen to stay in New Zealand as this pandemic unfolds partly because the daily word choices at U.S. press briefings we watch sow confusion and uncertainty. The lack of clarity, lack of respect for the voice of the experts, and lack of a clear plan causes us great concern. We feel safer here.

Words are powerful and serve you well when they support your intent. Your intent is founded in your values and can be influenced by your underlying beliefs. Being well connected to your values equates to being well connected to your heart. What is in your heart is the truth your brain seeks when formulating thoughts and words. Keep this path clear. Do the work necessary to create a clear pathway between your emotional sincerity and your thoughts and beliefs so that what comes out of your mouth truly represents you. When you experience this alignment, you will not have feelings like the following ones, and you will confidently choose your words well. You will feel into your words.

- *I should not have said that.*
- *I did not mean that.*
- *She took that the wrong way.*
- *He never gets me.*
- *I'm sorry I spoke up.*
- *I don't know what to say.*
- *Why did I say that?*

In Chapter One, we explored how your personal values inform your word choices. The stories, activities, and reflections guided you through connecting with yourself first and foremost. Doing so reinforces that the voice in your head is a choice. Only you have true power in making this choice. Others may have influenced the voice in your head with their words, but you get to choose the power those words will hold and if they align with your values. If not, reject them and stop playing them like a broken record or boomerang Insta pic.

In Chapter Two, we looked at the patterns that turn up with loved ones. You have the power to break conversation cycles that you have learned to expect and react to with your words. You are also a responsible member of the global village that influences our children. Your words frame their future. Ensure your words sow seeds of curiosity, praise, support and love. Use your voice to reinforce values for children and young adults whose hearing is sponge-like. Listen and speak as though one's success as an adult depends on it, because it might.

Chapter Three holds the key to choosing words well in situations that define us as humans. How we interact with those who are unlike us is driven by how we speak. We get to choose to contribute to our collective humanity when we listen more to the needs of others and teach ourselves to use words that have a positive impact. Every choice has at least two options. When we seek to understand more – more about ourselves, others, our inherent biases, how our beliefs inform our behaviors – we move closer to living our values.

Chapter Four is filled with work-related scenarios that present opportunities to consider word choices. Whether you are new to the workforce, about to retire from it, or somewhere in between, I suspect there were many examples that you can relate to. This section sets you up to listen for words differently as the receiver and reflect on how words might affect leadership and even business delivery. In the business world, words impact service delivery, change initiatives, team dynamics, difficult conversations, and your ability to influence others. Whether you are a leader or an employee, your words matter, and you get to use them to represent your values and connect you to your purpose at work.

In Chapter Five, I scratch the surface of other ways in which we communicate. In some cases, emojis, pictures, and symbols replace words. Our ability to communicate is expanding rapidly due to technological advances. By the time this book is published, there may be more venues. How we connect is another important choice. Each of us owns our message regardless of the format in which it is sent. As our options expand and our output shrinks (number of characters or use of an emoji), we are still obligated to get it right. Our choices should still be tied to our intent. When I wish to delight or celebrate another, I will choose to send a note in the mail. I will select words that bring the person joy that the champagne glass emoji cannot replicate.

I intentionally placed the chapter on how we connect with the universe at the end of the book. This chapter is the culmination of expression. To me, it represents how we show up every day. How we express who we are at our core. Each of us matters in the grand scheme, on this planet we call home. Our individual contribution to the world may be reflected in how we connect to a higher power. How we connect with others, as outlined in all the other chapters, determines how we show up spiritually. Are my words and actions aligned with my values? Do my beliefs support my values? Do I actively engage my heart and the thoughts in my head to inform what comes out of my mouth? Do I use my voice for the greater good of all? Do I intentionally express my gratitude? These are all questions steeped in a desire to do good in the world and be an active participant in humankind.

I once heard Deepak Chopra say that there are seven billion evolutionary paths on earth. I hope that yours includes self-compassion as well as empathy for others. Each of us possesses the ability to adapt. We are able to redirect our energy and improve our levels of awareness. There is so much we can do before we ever utter a word. We can choose to make compassionate connections and speak from our hearts.

Let us not consider this as 'have to do" hard work. Instead, make it "get to do" heart work. What words will you choose to support a loved one, or to gain a deeper understanding of the struggles of a co-worker? How are you using your voice to console during COVID-19? Who do you get to respectfully disagree with as you express your values? What are you learning about others as you ask powerful, open-ended questions? How will you use your words to protect someone against racial injustice? Yours is the voice of humankind. Speak your truth and maximize the power of your voice with well-chosen words.

Thank you for coming along on this exploration of word choices. I hope you will revisit sections that spoke to you. I invite you to return to activities and reflections that are part of your learning journey. You will find related videos and learning pathways at www.shortgroup. net. Personal growth through self-awareness is the greatest gift you can give yourself. I would love to hear about the impact this book has on your word choices. Please email me: Terre@shortgroup.net. I look forward to hearing how your words matter.

Acknowledgments

The word choices to describe the support I receive from my husband, James Short, are endless, yet none of them are enough. He has been my steadfast champion through 25 years of marriage. He is the love of my life. Our children, Erik and Taylor, support me with their unending search for truth through knowledge. I am so happy to learn from them and feel their love through everyday conversations. My husband and I both have extended families that we learn from daily, who have influenced my work directly or indirectly, which fills me with gratitude.

I am grateful my parents were high school sweethearts, which ultimately brought me into this world so I could fulfill my purpose. They have now been married 65 years! This book is a small part of why I am here, and I hope those who were a part of it will stick with me as I move along my evolutionary path.

Some of those inspiring individuals who appeared as I needed them are: Lisa Solis Delong, Laurie Huff, Frank Reed, Fran Jacques, Quint Studer, Pamela Herrmann, Margaret Stanzell, Margie Gilmore, Amy and Sandro Cima, Olivia Round, Lizz Marks, Hanna Kerns, Megan MacDonald, Kim Faith, Joan Houlton, Cheryle Maurer, Karen Somers, Deven Parlikar, and Lyn Ketelsen. If I missed anyone, please know it is a reflection of my memory, not my intent.

I am indebted to those who took the time to share their stories and content to reinforce the messages herein. I deeply appreciate their willingness to participate. They are: Davia Spain, Mike Baxter,

Michelle Saahene, Melissa DePino, Sarah Bowen, Sarah Henry, Surreina Gallegos Gerbman, Charlene Li, and Danielle Cook.

A special thanks goes to Colin Rolfe at Epigraph Publishing for his endless patience with my edits, style changes, and cover pickiness. He guided me through the process expertly and was always quick to answer my questions.

Finally, these words and all those that precede would not have met your eyes without two wonderful women in my life. Longtime friend, Kate Bridges, proofread several versions and taught me tons. I am forever grateful for how graciously she gave of her time and skill. My editor, DeAnna Carpenter, is a new light in my life and provided great support. She made the process joyful and she coined my new way of referring to what you now hold in your hands – my heartwork.

References

Alcoholics Anonymous. (2001). *Alcoholics Anonymous.* New York: A.A. World Services Inc.

Average Daily Time on Social Media. (2020, January 15). Retrieved from Broad Band Search: https://www.broadbandsearch.net/blog/average-daily-time-on-social-media

Awdish, Rana M. (2017). *In Shock, My Journey from Death to Recovery and the Redemptive Power of Hope.* New York: Picador.

Bowen, S. (2019). *Spiritual Rebel: A Positively Addictive Guide to Deeper Perspective and Higher Purpose.* Rhinebeck: Monkfish.

Brown, B. (2018). *Dare to Lead.* New York: Random House.

Brown, J. O. (2017). Leading With A "Yes, And." *Forbes.*

Carnegie, D. (2011). *How to Win Friends and Influence People.* New York: Simon & Schuster.

Coetzee, Melinde, N. M. (2006). The Relationship Between Personality Preferences, Self-Esteem and Emotional Competence. *SA Journal of Industrial Psychology,* 64-73.

Davis, H. F. (2017). *Beyond Trans Does Gender Matter.* New York: University Press.

Diangelo, R. (2018). *White Fragility: Why It's So Hard for White People to Talk About Racism.* Boston: Beacon Press.

Dorsey, J. R. (2010). *Y-Size Your Business.* Hoboken: John Wiley and Sons.

Eischen, T. (2015, Jan 4). Obama's Name for Cameron: Bro. *Politico.*

Eligon, J. (2018, Nov 13). Hate Crimes Increase for Third Consecutive Year. *New York Times*.

Erickson-Schroth, Laura, M. A. R. (2017). *You're in the Wrong Bathroom!* Boston: Beacon Press.

Faith, K. (2020). *Your Lion Inside: Discovering the Power Within & Live Your Fullest Life*. Charleston: Advantage.

Gendron, Tracey L., P. E. (2016). The Language of Ageism: Why We Need to use Words Carefully. *The Gerontologist*, 997-1006.

Gilliam, M. P. (2019). *Reviving Ophelia 25th Anniversary Edition: Saving the Selves of Adolescent Girls*. New York: Penguin.

Gottman, J. M. (2002). A two-factor model for predicting when a couple will divorce: Exploratory analyses using 14-year longitudinal data. *Family Process*, 83-96.

Greaves, T. B. (2009). *Emotional Intelligence 2.0*. San Diego: TalentSmart.

Grenny, Joseph, K. P. (2013). *Influencer: The New Science of Leading Change*. New York: McGraw Hill.

Harvard Business Review (2015). *On Emotional Intelligence*. Boston: Harvard Business School Publishing Corporation.

Harvard Business Review (2018). *Everyday Emotional Intelligence*. Boston: Harvard Business Review Press.

Heath, C. & D. (2017). *The Power of Moments*. New York: Simon and Schuster.

Henry, S. M. (2019). *Intricacies Are Just Cracks in The Wall*. New York: Still Poetry Photography.

Johnson, B. (2014). *Polarity Management: Identifying and Managing Unsolvable Problems*. Amherst: H R D Press.

Kimmerer, R. W. (2013). *Braiding Sweetgrass: Indigenous Wisdom, Scientific Knowledge, and The Teaching Of Plants*. Minneapolis: Milkweed.

Lee, Thomas H. (2016). *An Epidemic of Empathy in Healthcare – How to Deliver Compassionate, Connected Patient Care That Creates a Competitive Advantage*. New York: McGraw Hill.

Losada, M. A. (2004, Feb). The Role of Positivity and Connectivity in the Performance of Business Teams: A Nonlinear Dynamics Model. *American Behavioral Scientist*, 740–65.

Lucas, H. L. (1975). *The Memory Book*. New York: The Ballantine Publishing Group.

Marcus, H. R. (2008). Pride, Prejudice, and Ambivalence: Toward A Unified Theory Of Race and Ethnicity. *American Psychologist*, 651-670.

Mehl, Matthias R., S. V.-E. (2007). Are Women Really More Talkative Than Men? *Science*, 82.

Monahan, Leila, J. E. (2012). *A Cultural Approach to Interpersonal Communication*. Maldon: Wiley- Blackwell.

Mruk, C. J. (1999). *Self-Esteem 2nd Edition*. New York: Springer Publishing Company.

Patterson, G. M. (2012). *Crucial Conversations - Tools for Talking When Stakes are High*. New York: McGraw Hill.

Perez, S. (2018, October 30). *Twitter Doubling of Character Count*. Retrieved from Tech Crunch: https://techcrunch.com/2018/10/30/twitters-doubling-of-character-count-from-140-to-280-had-little-impact-on-length-of-tweets/

Rosenberg, Marshall. (2003). *Nonviolent Communication: A Language of Life*. Encinitas: Puddledancer Press.

Schutte, Nicola S., J. M. (2002). Characteristic Emotional Intelligence and Emotional Well-Being. *Cognition and Emotion*, 769-785.

Seamark, M. (2006, July 18). *Daily Mail*. https://www.daily-mail.co.uk/news/article-396408/Yo-Blair-What-words-plus-expletive-reveal-Bush-poodle-Blair.html

Selig, M. (2018). Six Ways to Discover Your Core Values. *https://www.psychologytoday.com/us*.

Seligman, Martin E. P. (2006). *Learned Optimism - How to Change Your Mind and Your Life*. New York: Vintage Books.

Singer, M. (2007). *The Untethered Soul*. Oakland: New Harbinger Publications.

Specter, E. (2019, November 1). *Carrie Bradshaw Getting Dumped Via Post-it Wasn't That Bad—By Today's Standards, Anyway.* Retrieved from Vogue: https://www.vogue.com/article/sex-and-the-city-carrie-berger-post-it-break-up

Spirituality and Practice. (n.d.). Retrieved from https://www.spiritualityandpractice.com/practices/practices/view/27383/prayer-to-mother-earth

Statista (2020, April 29). *COVID-19 deaths worldwide per one million population as of April 28, 2020, by country.* Retrieved from Statista: https://www.statista.com/statistics/1104709/coronavirus-deaths-worldwide-per-million-inhabitants/

Studer, Q. (2020). *The Busy Leader's Handbook.* New Jersey: Wiley.

Taylor, J. (2011). *Your Children are Listening: Nine Messages They Need to Hear From You.* New York: The Experiment.

Tochluck, S. (2010). *Witnessing Whiteness: I Need to Talk About Race and How To Do It.* Lanham: Rowman & Littlefield.

Vennet, M. V. (2015, March 12). *Epic Pew.* Retrieved April 21, 2020

Visual Capitalist (2019, October 02). *World Economic Forum.* Retrieved from weforum.org: http://www.weforum.org

Appendix

AIDET (Acknowledge, Introduce, Duration, Explanation, and Thank you). This framework is useful by any employee, including clinicians in direct communication with patients and their loved ones. Following it serves the purpose of reducing anxiety for those with whom you interact. In addition to patients, this works well within a team and with others in an organization.

SBAR (Situation, Background, Assessment, and Recommendation). This framework is typically used between clinicians. For example, when a patient is being handed over from one unit to another, or when a nurse is calling a physician regarding a patient.

TeamSTEPPS (Team Strategies and Tools to Enhance Performance and Patient Safety). The Department of Defense and the Agency for Healthcare Research and Quality developed this framework for the purpose of improving teamwork and communication.

Index

www.ingramcontent.com/pod-product-compliance
Lightning Source LLC
Chambersburg PA
CBHW021401090426
42742CB00009B/945